The Fundamental Basics of

Publishing a Book

Before Writing
During Writing
Organizing your
Interior
Book Covers
Uploading your
Files
Distribution
Marketing

Dr. Mia Y. Merritt

ISBN #978163173670-4

Other Books by Mia Y. Merritt:
The Cost of the Anointing
The Cost of the Anointing Workbook
Releasing Emotional Baggage
Prosperity is Your Birthright!
Prosperity is Your Birthright Workbook
Destined for Great Things!
Destined for Great Things Workbook
Words of Inspiration: Golden Nuggets for the Wise at Heart
Life After High School
Life After High School Workbook
All About the Military
Money and how it Multiplies
Money and how it Multiplies Workbook
Traveling The Road to Success
The Road to Inner Joy

Library of Congress Cataloging
in-Publication Data

Merritt, Mia

First Printing 2014
Printed in the U.S.A.

Introduction

Getting a book published is not as hard and cumbersome and some may think. Understanding the basics of the process is what helps to make the execution of your book smoother. Coming into the light of knowledge is key. For instance, knowing small, but relevant things such as how the title of a book on the spine must be faced to the left, knowing that all books must have an ISBN number in order to go on the book trade market, realizing that not all books have to be copyrighted, understanding that chapter titles should start on odd numbered pages, will help the book publishing process go so much easier for you.

It is also important to understand the difference between traditional publishing and self-publishing because many do not know. This book teaches you how to self-publish, but explains the difference between the two. In the traditional publishing process, an author submits a proposal or a manuscript to literary agents or editors in the hope that it will be selected for publication. If a work is selected, the publisher (usually) pays an advance to the author and negotiates a "rights" contract that transfers the publication rights from the author to the publisher. The publisher agrees to pay royalties to the author. This advance is a payment against future royalties. The publisher files the copyright with the government and provides the international standard book number (ISBN). The publisher also provides all editorial and production work without charge to the author. The publisher markets the book and seeks reviews in appropriate media. The publisher also takes on all risks of publishing the book and the author is required to cooperate in the marketing efforts.

When you self-publish, you are both the author and the publisher. You write your own book, secure your own ISBN, file your own copyright, take care of your own formatting, organizing, and editing and you do your own marketing and promoting. There is no advance that will be given and your royalty checks will be relatively small at first. You have control over what is written and you do not have to submit to any major changes in content, structure or even meaning when you self-publish.

Getting a major publisher to pick you up is not very easy. Major publishers usually target those who have a popular name, a reputation (good or bad) and the potential to sell books. More often than not, these people are approached by the publisher for their story. Other than that, you must gain some notoriety in order for a publisher to be interested in you. But be not dismayed! There have been many self-published authors whose books flew to the top of the Amazon and New York Times best seller list. You can be one of those people too, but you must know the fundamentals of successful book publishing. This book will teach them to you!

Overview

If you are reading this, it's because you are seriously thinking about writing a book, and I commend you on taking the first step. Most people desire to write a book, but never get around to writing it. Unfortunately, they die with at least one book inside of them and we never get a chance to have the benefit of reading what they were going to share with the world. Don't let that person be you.

Writing a book does many things for you; it increases your personal value, establishes you as an expert, and allows you to leave a legacy on earth. Therefore, when you give birth to your book, you want it to be a quality, professionally produced, information-packed book that will benefit its readers. As such, I have a few questions for you that will stimulate your thinking and will help catapult you to produce a quality literary project. My first question is,

✓ *What is your purpose for wanting to write a book?*

In answering this question, you must look at the content about which you seek to write.

✓ *Is your content going to be entertaining, informative, persuasive, educational, etc.?*

Once you identify that, your question will be easy to answer: i.e. "My purpose for wanting to write a book is to inform readers about..."

Before you begin writing, you must begin with the end in mind. In other words:

✓ *What is it that you want readers to have acquired or learned as a result of reading your book?*

✓ *What impact will your book have on readers?*

- ✓ *How will your book be unique from other books in its category?*

- ✓ *Are you able to state in one sentence what your book is about, such as: "This book is about how people can strategically use social media to enhance their businesses?"*

- ✓ *Can you convert that one sentence into a working question?*

Example: The working question here is, "What information must I give to readers on social media to help them enhance their business?"

- ✓ *Will your book be fiction (a children's book or a novel) or nonfiction (self-help, autobiographical, informational)?*

If non-fiction, it must be packed with useful, accurate, up-to-date and mind-stimulating information. If fiction, it should be creative, but compelling and interesting.

Where will you be getting information for your book (internet, interviews, personal experience, other books, articles, etc)?

The reason I have asked you these questions is because in order to produce a quality book, your answers to these questions must be readily available. If you cannot answer any of these questions, then you must seek to find the answers before embarking upon the writing part. The tips in each chapter of this book will help you with the logistics of putting your book together and will increase your knowledge and understanding of the book writing and book publishing process. Happy reading and then happy writing!

Table of Contents

Module 1
Before Writing
Preparing, Outlining, & Getting Organized

You can be the author without being the writer.
A ghostwriter can write your story for you. If you do not have the time or the clerical skills to write your own book, then you can hire a ghostwriter. As long as the ideas, thoughts, and story belong to you, then it is still YOUR book.

Ghostwriters are writers for hire who you pay to write your story, but they get none of the credit for the work they produce. You, as the author hire the "ghost" as a freelance writer to produce work for a set price. You take all the credit for the work produced by the ghostwriter. A ghostwriter may write books, articles, stories, reports, or other literary works that are officially credited to another person. They take your story, research, or information and write them in a way that makes them grammatically correct, publically acceptable, literary appropriate, and hopefully compelling and interesting to the readers. They make your information fitting for book form while maintaining your personality.

Many ghostwriters have written books for others that have made it to the New York Times bestseller list; and most ghostwriters have written books of their own. Steve Harvey hired Denene Millner to write his book 'Act Like a Lady...' Russell Simmons used Chris Morrow to write his book, 'Do You'. If you want to write a book, but you do not have the literary, English, or technical skills, you may want to consider this route.

When you do have the typing, grammar, formatting, organizing skills, you are in a position to do a lot of the necessary work yourself.

Module 1 Tip 2:
Make sure that your book is page balanced!
Make sure there are a proportionately balanced number of pages in each chapter of your book. A good balance would be something like this: Chapter 1: 9 pages; chapter 2: 7 pages; chapter 3:8 pages; etc. Not like this: chapter 1: 9 pages; chapter 2: 3 pages, chapter 3: 16 pages, chapter 4: 4 pages. Ideally, you would want all chapters to have an even number of pages, but that NEVER happens, so try to be as balanced as possible with three to four pages up or down.

If you do not have enough wording and essentially enough pages for a particular chapter, then you can consolidate the information into another chapter. Likewise, if you have too many pages for a particular chapter, then you can cut some information out and put it into another chapter. Ideally, you want the pages in your chapters to be as even as possible.

Module 1: Tip 3:
Set your margins and page size before you
begin writing.
If you have Microsoft Word (MS Word), you can work on your book from there. You do not need to purchase any fancy, expensive writing software just to put your words down. A good word processing program will work just fine. MS Word is NOT a typesetting program, but you can use its typefaces.

Before you start, set your page size (6x9, 5x8, 5.5x8, etc.). This will be the actual size of your book. Next, set your margins (1 inch all around, .7 inches all around, etc), insert your page numbers, and set your font styles before you begin writing a single word. If you already have your chapter titles, you may go ahead and even write those in, but that is optional.

When inserting your page numbers, roman numerals (i, ii,, iii, etc) are for the preliminary pages and standard numbers (1, 2, 3, etc) begin on Chapter 1; page 1. To set your page size, you go to "page layout" from the menu at the top left if working from MS Word 2007. Then you click on "size" to set the size of your book (5x8, 5.5x8.5, 6x9 etc). After you set the book size (which is also the page size), you set your margins by also going to the top left and clicking on "margins". Many books are one inch all around. However, I like to use .7 inches all around. It is neat, leaves room on all four sides, and gives you more writing space than one inch all around. This saves you more pages which ultimately saves you more money because the cost of your finished book will be determined by the number of pages you have. If your book does not have a lot of pages and you need it to look thicker, you may want to go with one inch all around. These dimensions are standard.

If you want will be a nonstandard sized book as in workbooks or children's books, you will have to customize the size in page layout area under "size" in MS Word. When you begin writing your book with the sizes and margins already set, you always know how many pages you have. You are typesetting as you write.

Module 1: Tip 4:
Make room for Your preliminary pages

As you begin working on your manuscript, do not begin writing on the very first page. The first few pages (about 10 pages) will be preliminary pages (introduction, dedication, foreword, etc) and some of those pages will be left blank. You need to account for those pages before you begin writing.

Module 1: Tip 5:
Always go with the current book-writing standard.

Over 400,000 books are published each year. Ninety-eight percent of those books are single spaced with a 12-point font. Double-spaced writing makes your work look old and dated. Standard writing is single-spaced 12-point font, although the font size may go up or down one size. Lately, authors have been increasing the font size in their books for those with vision issues. A font size that is 14 or higher is considered large print. You decide what you want based upon your targeted audience, but essentially, you want to go with the standard, which is between 10-12 point size. Children's book are going to have bigger font sizes. If you are writing a book that targets senior citizens, your font size would want to be bigger since vision diminishes as we get older. Reputable book publishers typically follow 'The Chicago Manual of Style: The Essential Guide for Writers, Editors, and Publishers' for book formatting. The Chicago Manual of Style is a style guide for American English published in 1906 by the University of Chicago Press. Its sixteen editions have prescribed writing and citation styles widely used in publishing. The Writer's Handbook is a writing guide for professional writers, publishers, editors, agents and broadcasters. Both of these books are widely accepted and used when publishing.

Keep in mind that when most people self-publish, they are not familiar with these writing standards, and they usually do their own thing when writing (bolding, underline, caps, etc.) which clearly shows the inexperience. Oftentimes in the writer's mind, they believe that their book will be acceptable, and in most cases, it probably will to the average reader, but a professional writer/editor/agent will look at the book and immediately know whether it was self-published or traditionally published. The key is for people to pick up your book and NOT know the difference.

Module 1: Tip 6:
Make sure that your content is updated and current.
(for nonfiction books)

If you are writing a non-fiction book (informational, biographical, textbooks, essays, documentary, etc.), be sure to research your topic thoroughly. You must be as current as possible and be sure there is a market for what you are writing. What category will your books be in (finance, self-help, Christianity, real estate, politics, children's books, motivation, technology, business, education, metaphysics, etc.)? Can you name at least five other books in your category? You will sell more books when your book is as specific as possible.

Module 1: Tip 7:
Giving Your Book a Title

People are attracted to books that have titles that are simple, easy to remember, and gives information that is appealing to them. See examples below:

- ✓ 15 Steps to Finding the Man of your Dreams
- ✓ How to become Rich in 90 days
- ✓ How to break a habit in 30 days
- ✓ A Survivor's Guide for Neophyte Attorneys
- ✓ A 30-Day Walk With God
- ✓ Starting a Business in 25 Easy Steps
- ✓ 15 pieces of advice you should never take
- ✓ 10 Basic Steps to…
- ✓ Six Beneficial Reasons to…

Module 1: Tip 8:
Begin your chapters and headings on odd pages
(the right side)

The very first page of your book falls on the right side. This will be your title page. On the back of that page is the left side. This is your copyright page. The page after that is on the right side. This page could be your acknowledgement, dedication, or introduction page; the page after that (left side) is left blank because it's the back of the previous page. The page after that will be on the right side, and can be your acknowledgement, dedication, or introduction page etc. Take notice that the only page with wording on the left side is the copyright page. All other pages with wording starts on the right side. That's because chapter pages or title pages should always start on the right side, which is an odd number page. If there is a page on the left with nothing written on it, you leave it blank and begin writing on the right side.

There are times however, when you will write on the left side, such as when/if your introduction, dedication or acknowledgement does not all fit on one page. In that case, you will continue writing on the back of that page (which is on a left side). To do that, is perfectly fine.

EXAMPLE:

If a chapter ends on this page, then start the next chapter on the very next page. Otherwise, this page is left blank.

6

Chapter pages should start on this side, which is an odd number page. If a chapter ends on this page, then the next page is left blank.

7

Module 1 Activity

1. Begin with the end in mind. What is it that you want readers to have acquired/learned as a result of reading your book?

_____

_____

2. What is your purpose for wanting to write a book? (to entertain, inform, amuse, teach, tell your story. etc.)

My purpose for wanting to write a book is to _____

_____

_____

3. In one sentence, what is your book about? For example: *"This book is about how people can strategically use social media to enhance their businesses."* _____

_____

_____

4. Convert that one sentence into a working question? Example: The working question here is, "What information must I give to readers on social media to help them enhance their business?" _____

_____

_____

*The content of your book is the response to your working question above. The answers to your working question are the reason for the existence of your book.

5. Write your main working question below (see module one activity). Example: The working question here is, "What information must I give to readers on social media to help them enhance their business?"

_____

_____

_____

* Make a list of secondary questions that come to mind from your main working question above. These secondary questions should answer the: who, what, when, where, why, and how. From those answers will develop your chapters. Think of as many secondary questions as possible because **the answers to these secondary questions will drive the content of your book.**

i. _____

_____

ii. _____

_____

iii. _____

_____

iv. _____

_____

v. _____

_____

vi. _____

_____

vii. _____

_____

viii. _____

_____

ix. _____

_____

x. _____

_____

6. Will your book be fiction (a children's book or a novel) or nonfiction (self-help, autobiographical, informational)? _____

* If non-fiction, it must be packed with useful, accurate, up-to-date and mind-stimulating information. If fiction, it should be creative, but compelling and interesting. Where will you be getting information for your book (internet, interviews, personal experience, other books, articles, etc)? _____

_____

7. How is your book *unique* from other books in its subject?

_____

_____

8. What kind of an impact will your book have on people? In other words, why would anyone want to buy your book or even read it for free if it doesn't give them some benefit, pleasure, enlightenment, solution, or meet their needs?_____

_____

_____

9. How many chapters do you think your book will have and why?

_____

_____

* In marketing and advertising, a **target audience**, is a specific group of people within the target market at which a product or the marketing message of a product is aimed. A target market is a group of customers that the author has decided to aim his or her marketing efforts for their book. A

well-defined target market is the first element to a marketing strategy.

* Target audiences are formed from different groups. For example: adults, teens, children, mid-teens, pre-scholars, scholars, men, women. To market to any given audience effectively, it is essential to become familiar with your target market, their habits, behaviors, likes, and dislikes.

Examples of a targeted audience:

Children
Young adults
Christians
Entrepreneurs
Doctors
Educators
Politicians
Housewives
Parent of Special Needs children
The Hearing Impaired
Athletes

10. Who is your targeted audience? _____

_____

11. Why is this your targeted audience? _____

_____

My Book Notes

Module 2
During Writing
Typesetting, Formatting & Content

Decide What Font to Write in

Decide what font you want your book to be written in. Writing in more than two fonts in the content of a book is considered unprofessional. Ideally, all of the writing should be written in one font style throughout, but chapter titles may have a different font and style. That is perfectly fine because titles are larger and should stand out. The most popular font styles are Times New Roman, Ariel, and Verdana.

In a printed book, a serif typeface is easier on the eyes. In typography, serifs are the small lines tailing from the edges of letters and symbols. A typeface with serifs is called a serif typeface. A typeface without serifs is called a sans-serif. Examples of serif typefaces are Times New Roman, Century Schoolbook, or Bookman old Style. If most of your books will be read on a computer screen, you may consider a sans serif typeface such as Arial, Tahoma, Verdana.

Module 2 Tip 2:
Preparing Your e-Book

You should already be thinking about an electronic version of your book, also known as an eBook. Once you have completed your printed book (Pbook), then the file from the Pbook will serve as your e-book (electronic book). The EBook is already completed once the Pbook is finished. That way, those who prefer to read online may read your book on their nooks, kindles, I-pads, computer, etc. You may also want to think about the audio book

(Abook) to target those readers who like to "listen" to books in their cars. Many people specialize in doing voice-carryovers for audio books.

Module 2 Tip 3:
Format consistency

Be sure there is consistency throughout your book when writing quotes, scriptures, excerpts, etc. For instance, if you have a quote on the chapter page in Chapter 1, then you should have a quote on the chapter page in every chapter of your book. For example:

1

PROSPEROUS PEOPLE PLAN FOR SUCCESS

> *The secret to productive goal setting is establishing clearly defined goals, writing them down and then focusing on them several times a day with words and emotions as if you've already achieved them.*
>
> *Denis Waitley*

If this is how you opened chapter one, then chapter two, should look something like this:

2

REMARKABLE MANIFESTATIONS APPEAR TO VISIONARIES

> *Keep your dreams alive. Understand to achieve anything requires faith and belief in yourself, vision, hard work, determination, and dedication. Remember all things are possible for those who believe.*
>
> *Gail Devers*

This way, each chapter opening is consistent with the other chapter opening in the book. If you end a chapter with a scripture or quote, then every chapter should end with a scripture or quote.

The first page of a new chapter ⬇

The end of a chapter ⬇

Chapter 2
Overcoming Obstacles
Success is to be measured
not so much by ...
~Booker T. Washington

You can start writing about here. Notice how the first line is indented?

Success Keys

* The successful life is a disciplined life.

* Self-reliant people rarely depend upon others to do for them what they can do for themselves.

Module 2 Tip 4:
Give People Credit When Quoting Them

When quoting someone, ALWAYS give them credit. When quoting a person from a book, the internet, a magazine, etc., be sure to cite the source. If you copy a sentence that you have read from another source, then you must write it as a quote and cite it appropriately. When you take a sentence from another source and write it as your own, that is blatant plagiarism, and diminishes your credibility and integrity. Most people are honored to be quoted, as long as you give them their credit.

Things that people say are not usually copyrighted or trademarked. It is usually something they have spoken in a conversation, an interview, or speech that is just being repeated. More than likely, you cannot be sued for quoted them, but when operating in integrity, you give credit where credit is due. If you do not know who said it, then you can say something like, *"I once heard the following quote…"* or *"It has been said…"* If quoting a poem and you do not know the author, then write "author unknown". You never want your integrity to be questioned in any aspect. If using entire sentences or paragraphs other than your own, you MUST cite the source (book, author, and year). Never write other people's work as your own. That is blatant plagiarism and you can be sued for that!

Module 2 Tip 5:
Snatch your readers' attention when they first begin reading your book.

If a book does not grab the reader's attention within the first few pages, it is not very likely they will finish it. Believe it or not, the attention span of adults is not that much different from children. If they are bored with your book in the beginning, then in their minds, that is a prelude of what the entire book will be like, so they put it down, never to pick it up again. Try doing one of the following below to snatch their attention.

1. Make a shocking statement in the very first sentence.
2. Open with a famous quote
3. Cite a quote from a source who is well-respected or (on the contrary) infamous or controversial
4. Ask a rhetorical question
5. Insert a shocking statistic
6. Use a shocking comment
7. Create a scenario that makes the reader think and wonder
8. Use an anecdote
9. Create an analogy
10. Make the first sentence of the first chapter something funny.

Module 2 Tip 6:
Be Creative When Writing Novels

Writing a novel is a creative process. You never know when a good idea might come to you, so you should always carry a notebook and something with which to write. You never know when and how you will be inspired, so keep your eyes and ears open and write down ideas for your novel as they come to you. Once you get all of your ideas on paper, it will be easier to see gaps that need to be filled.

Write a short summary of what your novel is about or what you want it to be about before you begin the actual writing process. Ex: *"A retired school principal finds his passion and embarks upon a new endeavor as a private investigator until he stumbles upon a deep, dark secret that could change life as he knows it."* This is the sentence that you will memorize when people ask you what your book is about. This sentence is the big picture.

Module 2 Tip 7:
Tips That Make Good Sentences for Novels

- ✓ Shorter is better. Eliminate as many words as you can. Be brief, concise and compelling.
- ✓ Write one sentence about your novel.
- ✓ Tie together the big picture with the personal picture.
- ✓ Read the one-line blurbs on the New York Times Bestseller List to learn how to do this. Writing a one-sentence description is an art form.

Expand your one sentence into a full-length paragraph describing the story setup, theme, plot, and ending of the novel. Just as a painter uses color and lines to create a painting, an author uses the elements of fiction to create a story.

Module 2 Tip 8:
Know the Main Elements of Novels

The main elements of fiction are character, plot, setting, theme, and style. Of these five elements, character is the *who*, plot is the *what*, setting is the *where* and *when*, theme is the *why*, and style is the *how* of a story.

You may find that you must go back and revise your one-paragraph summary a few times. This is good because it means that your characters are teaching you things about your story. It is inevitable that you will go back during the design process and revise earlier stages. The purpose of each step in the design process is to advance you to the next step. You can always go back and fix things when you understand the story better.

Module 2 Tip 9:
Break Your Story into Parts

This is the first thing you must do. In most cases, there are four primary parts to a novel that pushes it towards great recognition:

1. **PROBLEM:** Almost all novels have a major problem that needs to be solved. This is introduced near the beginning of the story and most of the story is spent trying to solve this problem.

2. **THEME**: Through solving the problem, an underlying idea, message, or moral is given by the author to the reader. This is called the theme.

3. **SETTING:** The problem is worked out in certain surroundings of place and time. This makes up the setting.

4. **PLOT**: What is done to solve the problem makes up the plot of the story. The plot, in its simplest form consists of:

    a. The action that gets the story off the ground, which is called the *motivating force* or *inciting incident*.

    b. After the story begins, difficulties are encountered. These complications make it more difficult to solve the problem.

c. When the greatest and usually the final difficulty appears, the story has reached its *climax*. This is usually the most exciting part of the book. The solution of the major problem usually occurs here.

d. After the climax, something usually happens before the very end that is not that exciting. This is the *anticlimax*. This is where an author usually ties up an loose ends.

e. The novel ends after the anticlimax with the *conclusion*.

5. **SUSPENSE**: Throughout the story, there are scattered incidents that keep up a strong feeling of curiosity as to what happens next. These elements of suspense have been used to keep you reading.

6. **CHARACTERS**: Novels may have both major and minor characters. The major characters large roles in the story. The minor characters are those that play small roles in the story, and are often used by the major characters to solve the problem. The author must bring the characters to life in the reader's mind.

It is important to note that different genres and stories require different types of character development. The characters in a novel usually represent a certain type of person. What character types will be represented in your novel?

Characters are usually judged by:

    i.   what they do
    ii.   what they say
    iii.   Their relation to other characters
    iv.   what the author says about them

In preparing to write your novel, it would be good for you to write a one-page summary sheet describes each of your major characters. You would want to include:

- ✓ The character's name and age
- ✓ The character's personality
- ✓ The character's motivation (what does he/she want abstractly?)
- ✓ The character's goal (what does he/she want concretely?)
- ✓ The character's conflict (what major part does this person play in the novel?)
- ✓ The character's epiphany (what will he/she learn and how will he/she change?
- ✓ A one-paragraph summary of the character's storyline

People who help to solve the problem in the novel and who are thought of as "good guys" are called protagonist. The characters that hinder the solution of the problem and are thought of as "bad guys" are called antagonists.

Will the protagonist have allies or enemies? Will they have a love interest? Will they be poor or rich? These are just a few questions that will be considered when writing your novel. These questions can be answered very quickly and early in the planning stage if you take the time to think the story through before you begin writing.

7. **PLOT:** Without a good plot, the novel is useless. Provide a sense of your main characters' motivations, especially those who will have conflict with one another. The plot is defined by conflict; either internal (coming to terms with the death of a child or the betrayal of a spouse for example) or external, (a stalker is watching through the window or the constant sexual harassment on the job by an immediate supervisor). The best plots are both original and interesting. The very best plots are defined by readers with the simple phrase, "*I*

couldn't put the book down." In other words, it was a great story. The plot outline for most novels have the following:

I.   Beginning:
Setting is established
Characters are introduced
The problem of the story is introduced

II.   Inciting Incident
Some big event gets the story "rolling". This is the motivating Force

III.   Complications
Events that make the solution to the problem more challenging and the story more interesting and suspenseful

8. **WRITING STYLE**: This refers to how the novel is written. It is the manner in which an author chooses to write to his or her audience. Writing style reveals both the writer's personality and voice, but it also shows how she or he perceives the audience. The choice of a conceptual writing style molds the overall character of the work. Is the writing style efficient or complex? Does the author use an extensive vocabulary or get straight to the point? Are words used appropriately with regard to meaning? Style should always be appropriate for the genre or story. An appropriate style adds to the texture of the novel; an inappropriate style does just the opposite.

Of course, basic writing rules apply to all types of writing styles. The following are some basic tips for novel writing:

✓ Limit the use of adverbs when describing dialogue: "he said angrily" should read, "he said...",

- ✓ avoid words that add unnecessary emphasis: "he was a little tired" should read, "he was tired," or "she was very thirsty," should read "she was thirsty"

- ✓ Avoid clichés like: "It was a dark and stormy night," use words appropriately and with their proper meaning, make the sentences clear and coherent, make them original without seeming to strain for originality.

- ✓ Most important of all, "SHOW" whenever possible, don't "tell." In other words, do not write: "Mike was angry." Show the readers his anger instead: *"Staring into the fire, Mike balled his hands into fists. Not this, he thought, anything but this!"*

Module 2 Tip 10:
Know the Different Types of Fiction

Literary fiction tends to appeal to a smaller, more intellectually adventurous audience. It leans towards complex sentences with original language. Thrillers tend to use shorter, more efficient sentences, especially as the pace quickens in the novel. What sets literary fiction apart is the notable qualities it contains such as excellent writing, originality of thought, and style that raises it above the level of ordinary written works.

Commercial fiction attracts a broad audience and may fall into any *subgenre* such as mystery, romance, legal thriller, western, science fiction, and so on. Written in a short, easy-to-read style, commercial fiction should be as mesmerizing to 15 year-olds as it is to 100 year-olds. Blockbuster commercial fiction authors include John Grisham, Sidney Sheldon, Danielle Steele, and Jackie Collins.

Mainstream fiction is a general term that publishers and booksellers use to describe both commercial and literary works that depict a daily reality that is familiar to most people. These books are usually set in the 20th or present-day 21st century and have a universal theme that attracts a broad audience at their core. Mainstream books deal with such myriad topics as family issues, coming of age initiations, courtroom dramas, career matters, physical and mental disabilities, social pressures, political intrigue, and more. Most of the novels that appear on the bestseller lists are considered mainstream.

9. **LENGTH:** How long is your book going to be? The length should be appropriate to the genre and appropriate to the story. Length is critically important in novels. Sometimes adding "bulk" is important to the overall pacing of a novel. If too much length is bad, so is a book or scene that is too short.

10. **CLIMAX:** As stated previously, when the high point of your story is reached, this is called the climax. There are five main elements to the flow of any good story: exposition, rising action, climax, falling action, and resolution. The climax is the high point of the action, and is often a turning point in terms of plot and the story's characters. It is where everything changes, and a new way of being is created, i.e. the problem is solved or all attempts to solve it finally fail. The climax is usually the most exciting part of the story, where the most dramatic action takes place.

The climax of a story should have readers on the edges of their seats. They should be breathless, tense, and curious!

11. **CONCLUSION:** Never close with a cliffhanger. Revealing the ending to your novel will not spoil the story for the readers. It will show that you have successfully finished your novel. Make sure every loose thread is tied up and never leave your readers guessing about anything. If your novel is going to be one of a series, then your ending can point to the sequel.

Module 2 Tip 11:
CHILDREN'S BOOKS

Children's books belong to a special category due to their formatting, color, pictures, and audience. Children's books are produced in color, but printing in color costs twice as much as printing in black and white, and printing color with offset ink printing is extremely expensive. Regular books are written in black and white. Book covers for standard books are in color, but the interior is in black and white. Children's books do not command a high price, but the market for children's books is huge. The publishers are swamped with submissions and the $20,000+ production cost is a huge investment. However, according to sales rank express, people buy 3.1 billion dollars worth of children's books each year. Most children's books sell for an average of $7.34 in soft cover and $14.51 in hardcover. It is hard to make money off children's books when four-color printing is so expensive and the minimum press run is 3,000 books.

Module 2 Tip 12:
THE LAYOUT OF CHILDREN'S BOOKS

It is highly recommended that children's books be laid out in PowerPoint. This multimedia program allows the addition of video, animations, sound, and hot hyperlinks leading to more information. The children's book can be interactive and the child may click on icons for more information, a different story line, animations, and sound.

The website below is an excellent source for a potential author wishing to write a children's book:

> http://www.dummies.com/how-to/content/writing-childrens-books-for-dummies-cheat-sheet.html

The website below takes you step by step on how to write a children's book:

> http://thepioneerwoman.com/blog/2011/04/twenty-steps-to-writing-a-childrens-book/

Module 2 Tip 13:
Age Appropriate Children's Books

Consider which age group interests you as a writer. The term "children's books" covers everything from board books with one word on a page to chapter books, novels and non-fiction factual books written for students in middle school and teens in high school (young adults). Needless-to-say, the plot, content, and themes of your book must be age appropriate for your intended readers. Keep in mind that parents are the ultimate gatekeepers who determine whether a child reads your book or not.

Module 2 Tip 14:
Five Things to do in Preparing to Write a Children's Book:

1. Have an interesting child or an inanimate object as your main character. The book should be about the child themselves or from a child's perspective. The child should be instrumental in working out the solution or solving the conflict.

2. Think about the character or animal around which the book will be centered. It could be about a rabbit or a butterfly, a lonely elephant, or a sad butterfly. Also, find a simple setting that a child could understand or relate to. It could be fictional because children will most likely believe it.

3. Think of a simple event or conflict, such as a rainstorm or getting all muddy after the rain, getting lost, feeling left out, etc.

4. A children's picture book is 22 pages on the average. Allow four pages for preliminary pages (copyright, introduction, dedication, etc.) You then have about 17 pages to work with. Write tightly and with concrete words that evoke concrete

images. Use words that are closest to the senses: taste, touch, smell, hearing, seeing.

5. Always end the story on a happy note, no tears: Now the family is back, the rabbit is reunited, realizes he belongs best at his very own home, and gets cookies as a treat for coming home safe.

Module 2 Tip 15:
Poetry Books

We have talked about fiction, non-fiction, and children's books, but for those interested in writing poetry books, you must consider the fact that you must have enough poems to make a book. Let's say you have 50 poems written. Although 50 poems may seem like a lot, you must remember that one page is actually two pages, because pages in a book are back-to-back. So essentially, you would have 25 pages of poems, which would be a small, but doable book. When you add your preliminary pages and maybe some pages in the back, there are about 30-35 pages. Some companies will not even print your book if it's not a certain number of pages, but when you self-publish you can do anything you want to - within reason and within professionalism that is. So keep that in mind.

Module 2 Tip 16:
Get Creative with Your Poetry Book

If you have 50 poems, you may get creative and mix your poetry book with other information or stories in order to fill up the pages. In other words, you would categorize your poems first. Then you could do some research on the subject that your poems are about. Write about the information you researched, then give a few pages of poems at the end (or at the beginning) of your chapter or section. You would then go to the next subject, give readers good, meaningful information on that subject, then end the chapter with a few of your poems. That way, you are filling up the pages in your book, but your content is still useful. You have a mixture of both poems and information.

Below are some Q&A on publishing poetry books. This information comes from www.poets.org. Please visit that website for more information on publishing poems.

- **How can I become a poet?** The best advice for writing poetry is to read lots of contemporary and classic poetry. Read literary journals and magazines geared toward writers as well.

- **How can I get my poems published?** Start small. Everyone wants to publish a book, but you should be aware that most writers start their careers by submitting their work to literary magazines and journals, gaining recognition from editors, agents, and peers. After your work has appeared in a variety of periodicals and you have amassed a solid manuscript, try approaching small presses and university publishers. There are also several well-respected first-book contests, including the Walt Whitman Award, which you could enter.

- **Where should I submit my poems?** Research is pivotal. Spend some time finding journals and 'zines online or in print that publish work that you enjoy or is similar to your style. *Poet's Market*, published annually, is an essential sourceBook for poets interested in sending out their work. It contains listings of publishers with descriptions, contact information, and submission guidelines. *Poets & Writers* magazine, published six times per year, is another excellent resource.

- **Is rejection a bad sign?** Dr. Seuss' first book, '*And to Think That I Saw It on Mulberry Street*' was rejected 27 times before it received a "yes" and was finally published in 1937. One of his most famous rejection letters read, *"This is too different from other juveniles on the market to warrant its selling."* During his lifetime, Dr. Seuss has won two Academy Awards, two Emmy Awards, the Pulitzer Prize and a Peabody Award. He sold over two million books including some of his most popular: The Cat In The Hat, The Sneetches, Green Eggs & Ham, Oh, The Places You'll Go, and How The Grinch Stole Christmas. Had he given up after the 26th rejection, he never would have reached his prize, so is rejection a bad sign? NO! Not at all!

It is important to be patient, yet tenacious, when trying to publish your work. Do not be discouraged by rejection. A hand-written, personal rejection from a good publisher is far better than an acceptance from a bad one. Many writers who are now well-known earned nothing but rejections for years. When a poem or manuscript comes back from one publisher, submit a fresh copy to the next one on your list.

- **Do I need an agent?** No. You can submit your work to journals and small publishing houses on your own. In fact, very few poets ever work with agents. However, the big publishing houses - the ones whose books you see in every bookstore publish very little poetry at all. Many good agents, meanwhile, will not even return your call unless you have already published a book.

- **How do I format my submission?** There are eight steps below you may take to keep your poems out of the recycling bin:

    1. Read the publication (or samples of the publisher's offerings) *before* you send your work to them. Make sure they publish the kind of poetry you are sending. You don't want to waste your time or theirs.

    2. Request submission guidelines from the publisher and adhere carefully to them.

    3. Always enclose a self-addressed stamped envelope for a reply. If you request your work returned, make

sure to include a large enough envelope with adequate postage.

4. Unless guidelines specify otherwise, send only three to five poems.

5. Choose a standard typeface that is clean and easy to read. (See Module 2 Tip 1). Twelve-point Times New Roman is a reliable choice. Do not use a script-style font (*Edwardian Script*, *Monotype Corsiva*, *Kunstler Script*) .

6. Make sure that whatever you send is *perfect*! Have a reliable person proofread your work. Check the spelling of the address, especially if you are sending it to a particular person's attention.

7. Keep your cover letter short: your bio should take up only a few lines; do not explain your poetry; it should speak for itself; do not ask for or expect to receive feedback on your work.

8. Be aware that it often will take a while for publishers to respond. Be patient. Do not call unless it is to inform them that your work has been accepted by another publisher.

Module 2 Tip 17:
Tips on Writing Poetry Books

Below are some tips to help you get started if you desire to write a poetry book.

1. Get all your poems typed on the computer. Most people have their poems written on paper in a notebook.

2. Decide what size you want your book to be. If you have more than 60 poems, that is a good size for a chapbook (book of poems).

A 5x8 would be a nice book size for this number of poems.

3. Categorize your poems by subjects, categories, or themes and put them in separate piles i.e. a broken heart, falling in love, confidence, never giving up, holidays, family, loneliness, etc.
4. Once your poems are organized and in the order you want them to be read, choose a title for your poetry book. A title may have suggested itself during your sifting of the poems, perhaps the title of a central poem, a phrase taken from one of the poems, or something completely different.

5. Be sure you carefully proofread all of your poems or have an editor do it once the book is in the order you want it. Pay close attention to each poem, each title, each line, each punctuation mark. You will likely find yourself making additional revisions to your poems. When in doubt about punctuation or line breaks, read the poem aloud.

6. Once your interior is ready and your covers are done, follow the submission steps in module 5 of this book.

If you want to submit your poems in poetry contests, see the websites below:

Poetry contests:
http://poetry.about.com/od/contestlinks/Contest_Links.htm

For a list of poetry publishers, see the website below:
http://welcome.friesenpress.com/main/poetry/confidence/adwords/poetrynew- a/poetry+publishers?gclid=COL5m-nhk7UCFQiqnQodLAUAZA

http://www.abbottpress.com/LP02F01C008.aspx?CAT=PPC&LS=SearchEngine&SRC=Google&GKW=Poetry-Misc&KW=z_Poetry&utm_source=google&utm_medium=cpc&utm_campaign=poetry&gclid=CLOehvbhk7UCFQixnQodQgsAHg

http://poetry.about.com/od/poetrypublishers/Publishers_Online_Poetry_Catalogs.htm

Module 2 Tip 18:
Get all of Your Ideas Out of Your Head!

As you are getting your thoughts out of your head and on to your paper or computer, do not worry about grammar, spelling and punctuation initially. Getting your thoughts and ideas out of your head and onto your computer screen is the main idea. Everything pertaining to your book that is in your head must come out. Just write, write, and write some more or type, type and type some more! You will find that as you position yourself each day at the same time to write, the spirit of inspiration will meet you, and will give you creative and unique ideas for your book. Thoughts and ideas will begin to flood your mind and you will find that you will not be able to write or type fast enough. If you are not consistent, persistent, and committed to writing your book, you will frequently get writer's block and that can be frustrating. The key is your consistency and commitment to your literary project.

Module 2 Tip 19:
Save your Work!

Keep your working manuscript in at least two places: on your computer (or laptop), and on a USB drive (thumb drive). Before you retire for the day, save what you have done in BOTH places. That way, if your computer crashes or the jump drive breaks (God forbid), you have a backup. Some people even email themselves the last version of their work. It does not matter how you back up your work, as long as you back it up. There is nothing worse than losing all your work because you did not have a backup.

Module 2 Tip 20:
Include your Contact Information in your Book

Always have a page in your book with your bio and contact information (website, email address, phone, etc.). This may be in the front or back of the book. Some call it the 'About the Author' page. This is the page where you can put a headshot of yourself if it's not already on the front cover. Depending on the book, you may want to include resource information, discussion topics, or a mini glossary if applicable. Some have an order form in their book to order directly from them. In the back of "some" of my books, I have what's called, 'Discussion Topics for Book Clubs'. This section lists topics/questions that can guide a discussion after the book has been read. You can do this as well depending upon the topic of book you have written. If it is a "how to" or informational book, you may have a 'FAQ' section or a 'Facts About...' section.

Module 2 Tip 21:
Insert your Preliminary Pages

When you have finished writing the content (also known as your interior), which is the biggest part, go back and write your preliminary pages which may include your introduction, acknowledgements, dedication, foreword, Table of Contents, Epilogue (epilogue goes in the back) etc. If you have a foreword, make sure you spell FOREWORD correctly because many misspell it. You do not need all of those pages listed above, however. The standard is usually the introduction, dedication, and table of contents. Authors who have forewords written for them, usually do so by people who have made a name for themselves.

As mentioned, your preliminary pages are written in roman numerals (I, ii, iii etc), and include all the pages before chapter one starts. Preliminary pages may include the following:

Title page: (recommended) The very first page of the book. It is simply a page where the title of your book is written in large font with your name as the author under the title.

Copyright Page: (mandatory) Goes directly behind the title page with the copyright symbol and the year the book was published i.e.: ©2014

Dedication Page: (optional) Not all books have this, but many do. Some dedicate their books to their spouses, their mentors, their children, in memory of loved ones, or even to their readers. It's all up to you as the author.

Introduction Page: (recommended for non-fiction books, but not necessarily for novels or children's books) You always want an introduction page unless the book is very small, as in a book of quotes, a children's book, or a novel. The introduction gives readers a preview of the book's content. It may talk about how the book came into fruition, may give background information on the subject of the book, etc. Essentially, the introduction page gives readers a preview of what the book is about.

Acknowledgement Page: (optional) Not all books have this. This is a page where you thank those who helped you with your book. If you had a team of individuals help you put the book together, then it may be nice to acknowledge them. Some acknowledge their editor, book consultant, spouse, etc.

About the Author Page: (recommended) This can go in the back or the front. I usually see it in the back. It is a short bio about you and lists your contact information here.

Table of Contents: (recommended for non-fiction books, but not for children's books) This should always go before the first chapter.

Module 2 Tip 22:
Proofreading your Chapters

After you have finished writing a chapter and you are pretty confident that it says all that you want it to say, then start writing the next one. Do not immediately proofread the chapter you just wrote because it is too fresh in your head and you will NOT see any errors you may have made. You will read what you know you wanted to say verses what is actually there. Begin writing your next chapter and concentrate only on perfecting that one. After you have written the next chapter or two, *then* go back to the first one to proofread it. By then, it will not be as fresh and you will read what is actually there, rather than what you know you were trying to say. Go on writing chapter three, then proofread chapter two and so on. You may also write all of the chapters, then wait until the end to proofread everything. It is totally up to you, but the key is to proofread. No one is so good that they can just write without proofreading.

Everything must be proofread from front to back - including preliminary pages. Errors will be found and necessary changes will be made. You may copy and paste, edit, delete, add, modify, rephrase, etc. This is when you need to correct misspelled words and sentence structure. THERE WILL BE ERRORS AND CHANGES!

Once you have done your part, pass the manuscript over to a professional wordsmith to check the grammar, syntax, style, punctuation, and spelling. No writer is so good that they can skip editing. Invest in a good editor! After an editor returns your manuscript, reread it to make sure they have not changed your context or meaning in the book an that they have not introduced any new mistakes.

**One thing that will turn readers off from your book real fast is a lot of misspellings, punctuation errors, endless paragraphs, run-on sentences, empty rhetoric, no organizational flow, and nonsense!

Writing a book establishes you as an expert in the subject in which you are writing. Becoming an author stands you out as an accomplished individual. The last thing you want to do is produce a book infested with spelling, grammatical and punctuation errors. It can do more harm to your reputation than good.

Module 2 Tip 23:
Consider Having a Focus Group Get-together
Once you feel that your book is finished or almost finished, you may want to have an excerpt-reading party or focus group get-together where a few of your closest friends and family will come over and read "excerpts" from your book and give you constructive feedback and suggestions about it. They also will be able to point out any errors. Keep in mind that the purpose of this is to help you produce a professional product, therefore you must be open to receiving

constructive criticism. If you cannot handle constructive criticism, then do not do this. If you are willing to do it, then you are able to make any changes they may find before having your book printed for the first time.

Module 2 Activity

1. What size book do you think will work for you?

___ 6x9 (standard)   ___ 5.5 x 8. (standard)
___ 5x8 (standard smaller)

___smaller than these sizes   ___ larger than these sizes

2. What do the following stand for?

EBook: _____

Pbook: _____

Abook: _____

HBook: _____

3. What are you going to say or do to snatch your readers' attention when they begin reading your book? _____

_____

_____

_____

4. What do you think you will have a consistency of throughout your book? It could be in the beginning or at the end of each chapter. ___quotes ___scriptures

___poems   ___statistics ___lessons learned
___other ___ nothing other_____

5. Do you have a title for your book yet? If so write it here:

_____

If not, list some key words that you may want in your title. You may also have a "working title" for your book. Key words:

_____   _____

_____   _____

6. People buy books based upon three things. What are those three things:

    i. _____

    ii. _____

    iii. _____

7. You should always have a backed up current version of your work. What two places will your most current work be?

    i. _____

    ii. _____

8. If you are thinking about writing a novel, then write in a short summary (2-3 sentences) what your novel will be about.

_____

_____

_____

9. What will be the main problem in your novel?

_____

_____

_____

10. Where will the setting take place?

_____

_____

_____

11. What will the plot be? _____

_____

_____

_____

12. What will the theme be? _____

_____

_____

_____

13. Who will the main character(s) be?

_____

_____

_____

14. Who will be some of the minor characters ?

_____

_____

_____

My Book Notes

_____

_____

_____

_____

_____

_____

_____

_____

_____

_____

_____

_____

_____

_____

_____

_____

_____

_____

_____

_____

_____

_____

Module 3
Organizing Your Interior Pages
Be sure there is consistency of formatting throughout of your book

Spacing and Formatting

Be sure that spacing and formatting are consistent on each page and that paragraphs are indented appropriately. If a paragraph only contains three or four sentences, it should be combined with another paragraph. You must also decide early on what font you want to write your book in. Twelve-point is the standard, but as mentioned previously, more and more writers are starting to write their books in larger size fonts. Some books are written in 14 point and a few are written in 10 point. My suggestion is to always go with the standard, which is a 12-point font. If you increase the standard by .5, making it a 12.5 size, it will not be noticeable. That is something to consider as well.

This is a **12** point font. It is the standard size. Most books are written in this size.

This is a **12.5** size font. It is a wee bit bigger than a 12 point.

This is a **13** size font, one size larger than the standard. It is not too big and not too small.

This is a **13.5**, a little big for a standard book.

This is a **14**, which is considered large print. Unless you are writing for a group of elderly people or children, I would stay away from this size.

Keep in mind that just because you may have problems seeing a standard size does not mean that your readers do. You are writing for the benefit of your readers, not yourself. However, when your book is for electronic purposes, you must increase the font size because the cover is seen in thumbnail catalogs and they are relatively small. Essentially, the book is already ready to be converted into an e-book once the paperback is done. For the e-book, all you would need to do is increase the font size.

Module 3 Tip 2:
Important Reminders

There is no space needed between paragraphs; they can fall on top of each other, but there should be a space between the end of a line and a new subtitle. Subtitles should not be in all caps, but they can be in bold. This is when using bold is appropriate.

Important Reminders:

- Do not underline words to emphasize them. Justify the text.
- Use BOLD CAPS within the content of your writing *sparingly*.
- Do not use the word "by" on your front cover
- Do not start chapters on the left side of the page.
- Do not use more than one font style in your text (this does not include chapter titles or the title of your book)
- Do not use Excessive Punctuation!!!!! This will not create a greater sense of urgency or strong emotion, especially in formal writing. BIG NO-NO!
- Do not use too many contractions (don't, won't didn't). Try to spell out the words as much as you can. However, there are some sentences where the contractions have a better flow. In those cases, *it's* fine to use them. Use contractions sparingly.

Module 3 Tip 3:
Underlining and bolding

Underlining and bolding throughout a book is considered unprofessional and is a dead give-away that the author self-published and had no knowledge of professional writing guidelines. I have used bolding in some of my books, but very scarcely. If you want to emphasize something, put it in italics, but too much italics is not good either. Too much bold, italics, and/or underlining conveys that you are an amateur writer unfamiliar with the proper book-publishing standard.

Module 3 Tip 4:
Endorsements for your Book

If you are interested in having endorsements/blurbs, you will need to leave a few additional blank pages in the front of your book in addition to the other preliminary pages. These pages will be filled in later by people you ask to write a recommendation for your book. If you leave the pages blank, then you will not have to reformat your book; so when you plug in the testimonials, it will not throw the page numbers off.

Before you upload your manuscript (covers and interior) to the company you are using, you may send a chapter or two to the people you would like to endorse your book. You may actually do this while you are still writing the book. That way, when your book is finished, you will have all of the testimonials in. In other words, if you have completed five chapters in your book, you may send one of the chapters (in PDF format) to people for them to read before the book comes out and ask them to write a recommendation based upon what they read. By the time your book is complete, you should have all of your testimonials in. Testimonials should be no more than two or three lines - no more than that.

If you request someone to write a foreword for your book, leave a full page for them to write. The person who writes the foreword is usually a well-known person, so they get a complete full page to write (and the back of that page if necessary). You must know exactly where everything will be plugged and leave those pages blank until you are ready to fill them in.

Examples of Endorsements/Recommendations:

This book is an excellent reminder of how much God loves us and how He is waiting to bless us! Prosperity is Your Birthright is a foundation for becoming all you can be with God's help. Read it, relish it and be blessed!

Rev. Dr. Jimmy Brown
Radio Talk Show Host, Hot 105 "Hot Talk"
Former Chief of Police Metro Dade Police Department

I was so intrigued by this book that I began practicing some of the new principles immediately. I could see the practicality in each principle, and realized that they only took a degree of self-discipline to apply. For the person who desires to take their lives to the next level, this book is a must read.

Dr. Venessa Walker, Chiropractic Physician
Health Wellness Speaker

Dr. Merritt's book gives practical, everyday strategies for reaching success. Her simplistic, yet profound principles will work in the life of the determined, if you work them. This book is a must read for people from all walks of life!

Dr. Jaffus Hardrick, Vice President
Florida International University
Division of Human Resources

Mia's book is a very inspirational, easy to follow road-map to spiritual and worldly success. She takes her teachings from biblical principles and uses those principles as the foundation to which all success, prosperity, and wisdom are acquired. This book is a must read!

Dr. Alberto Rodriguez
Superintendant Amherst Regional Public Schools

Module 3 Tip 5:
Know What Goes on the Back Cover of Your Book

Your back cover will contain your most important selling points. The back cover of your book is where you write what your book is about. Some write things such as: "Reading this book will help you to learn/acquire/develop/understand, _____." Since you cannot write all this on the front cover, it goes on your back cover in a small paragraph or bullet points. This is where your picture may go as well if it's not on the front cover of your book.

Module 3 Tip 6:
Cover Art for Front, Back & Spine

You will need cover art for your book for online promoting. If you are an artist, you might be able to create a first-class book cover yourself. There are also subsidy publishers such as Lulu (www.lulu.com) and Booktango (www.booktango.com) that have stock art and cover layout templates. For a professional-looking cover, you should work with a graphic designer. They are skilled professionals and know where each element of a cover should be placed. Money invested in your covers will pay off in sales.

You do not have to wait until after you write your book to create your covers or book layout (front, back & spine). You may begin working on those things before you start writing or even during the book-writing process. Perhaps one of those days when you are having writer's block, you may work on your covers or contact a graphic designer when you are halfway or three-fourths finished with the book. The graphic designer can be working on your covers while you are still writing the book.

Module 3 Tip 7:
How to Insert Headers

Not all books have headers, but if you do, make certain that they are inserted correctly. Headers do not go on chapter pages. They begin on the page after the chapter page, which should be on an even numbered page. Headers for even pages are left flushed. Headers for odd pages are right flushed. You decide what you want on your headers. Most people have the title of the book as a header for every even numbered page and the chapter title for every odd numbered page. This is entirely up to you. It is important to keep in mind however, that not all books have headers.

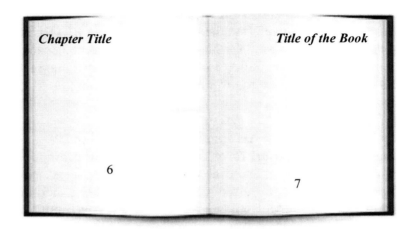

Module 3 Tip 8:
Table of Contents Page

After you have finished writing, proofreading and editing, make sure that your Table of Contents page matches your chapter titles and preliminary pages. Make sure that all chapters start on the right side (odd numbered page). When you start making changes to the interior by adding and deleting things, this can change where things fall on pages, so you must cross check again with the Table of Contents and page numbers. Adding or deleting things can push pages down or bring things up, so be sure that a chapter page has not been pushed down to an even numbered page. If so, you must leave the even page blank, then start the chapter on the next page. That is why you wait until everything is finished before adding headers and cross-referencing pages with the Table of Contents.

On one of the last few pages of your book, you may include listings of other books you recommend or other products you also available for readers to buy. On this page, you can also inform readers of the different versions in which your book is available (workbook, eBook, pbook, abook, etc) and you should send readers to your website (if applicable).

Example:

Books Written by
Dr. Mia Y. Merritt

Module 3 Activity

1. The size font that my book will be written in is _____
   because _____

   _____

2. I have decided to:

   ___have headers in my book
   ___no have headers in my book
   ___ undecided

3. Who will design the cover for your book?

   ___ a graphic artist
   ___ someone I know who is very artistic
   ___ I will design it myself
   ___ not sure yet.

4. Where (if at all), will your professional headshot go in your book?

   ___ front cover ___ front inside ___back cover ___ back inside
   ___ I don't want my picture anywhere in my book

5. Will you have endorsements for your book? _____

6. Will you have someone to write a foreword for your book?

   _____ ? Do you know who as yet? _____

My Book Notes

_____

_____

_____

_____

_____

_____

_____

_____

_____

_____

_____

_____

_____

_____

_____

_____

_____

_____

_____

_____

Module 4
Book Covers and Logistics
Knowing all the parts of your book

Regardless of what is said, people do judge a book by its cover. The cover is the first thing people are drawn towards when they pick up a book. A good cover will draw in potential readers, whereas a poorly designed, ugly or boring cover will cause people to overlook the book and not even consider picking it up. The bottom line is that your cover needs to be an attention-grabber! It needs to stand out among other books within its genre.

Module 4 Tip 2:
Parts of a Book Cover

Your book has two main parts: the <u>interior</u> (content) and <u>exterior</u> (book cover). Your book cover has three parts: the <u>front cover</u>, the <u>back cover</u> and the <u>spine</u>. The wording on the spine should always be facing to the left. Ideally, your covers should reflect the message of your book's content, but that is not always the case. A good cover should be not only pleasing to the eye in terms of the color scheme, but it should be evocative of its topic and theme. As stated before, but bears repeating, do not write the word "by" on your front cover. Ex. by Mia Merritt. This is a no-no! Just write your name. It is automatically understood that you are the author if your name is on the front cover. **This is a no-no!** ↓

Spine ⬇

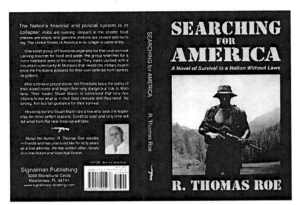

Back Cover ➡   ⬅ Front Cover

The wording on the spine always faces ⬆
the left.

Your book cover should do three things:
1. Advertise your book
2. Showcase you, the author
3. Set the "feel" of what's inside your book

*Important note: Although you need an eye-catching appealing book cover that will draw people to your book, you also want the content of your book to be filled with meat and potatoes. It's very disappointing to have bought a book with an awesome cover and the inside is filled with worthless rhetoric.

Module 4 Tip 3:
Your Cover Art should be portable
Your cover artwork should be provided in both jpg and pdf formats and should be usable for fliers, business cards, and in other promotional ways. It should be able to be uploaded to social media sites and even placed in your email signature. Your Pbook (printed or paperback) will require a full cover (front, back & spine). Your eBook will only need a front cover. As I mentioned before, you may design your bound book covers at lulu, blurb, or createspace (all end in .com). For eBooks, you must increase the font size of your title

and subtitle because the cover is seen in thumbnail catalogs, which are relatively small.

There are software programs that can assist you with designing your book covers. In-design and Quark are the more popular book creating programs or you can do it the old fashion way: Design three separate documents: the front, the back, and the spine, but if you do it this way, you must leave room for a bleed. In other words, if your book is a 5x8, then you must set your size at 5.75x 8.75. If it is a 6x9, then you would set your sizes for 6.75x9.75. You must always leave room for a bleed, which is room to roll over and cover white spots if necessary.

Some people even get matching bookmarks and/or pens to go with their books and they give them out as promotional items when people buy their book, but that's after the entire book-writing process is finished. You may also go online and find nice images for your book. Some are free, some you pay for. www.photos.com has a nice variety of photos from which to choose. There are also some nice images to choose from in Google images.

Module 4 Tip 4:
You will need an ISBN Number

In order for your book to get published and go on the book distribution market, you will need two things: an International Standard Book Number (ISBN) and a barcode. An ISBN is a ten or thirteen-digit number assigned to every book before publication. This number identifies you as the author and it identifies the book. The number always traces back to the author.

Barcodes help track sales of products. The main usage of a barcode is to identify an item. A barcode is a series of vertical black lines with white spaces in between. The most common bar code is called a Universal Product Code or UPC. Notice the ISBN is indicated on each of the barcodes below. Prices listed on barcodes are optional.

You cannot use the same ISBN number for different versions of a book. For example, you will need one ISBN for a paperback, a different ISBN for your eBook, a different one for the hardback, etc. Even though the book's content may be the exact same, you still need different numbers for each different version of your book. The ISBN identifies the different version. In other words, one ISBN number may identify my book 'Prosperity is Your Birthright' as a hardback, another ISBN may identify the same book as a paperback and still another ISBN may identify the eBook version. The number is 13 digits long if assigned after January 1, 2007, and 10 digits long if assigned before 2007. Your ISBN is going to be 13 digits long.

You can get 10 ISBNs for $275.00 or 100 for $575.00 from Bowker (the name of the company) at https://www.myidentifiers.com/isbn/main. If you only want to buy one number for now, you may find one for as low at $20.00 at http://www.isbnservices.com/. Do not pay more than $30.00 for a single 13-digit number. You do not always have to buy a barcode because many of the companies that print or publish books will automatically assign you one. Just focus on the ISBN number initially, not so much the barcode. Your ISBN number will go on your copyright page, and will automatically be placed on the barcode.

Homework: Pick up some books around you and identify the ISBN number on the copyright page. No book can ever be published without this number.

Module 4 Tip 5:
Copyright Your Work

Whenever you write a book, article, dissertation, publication, or anything that will be made public, it is considered your "intellectual property" and you should want to protect your property by having it copyrighted. If you do not copyright your work, then anyone may come along and take credit for what you did. They may actually steal your work and have YOUR WORK copyrighted as theirs if you have not copyrighted your own work. Copyrighting is a form of protection grounded in the U.S. Constitution and granted by law for original works of authorship. Copyrighting protects both published and unpublished works. You really do not need to copyright an autobiography, because no one has your identical story.

Below are some frequently asked questions (FAQ) about copyrighting. These FAQs come directly from the copyrighting website.

WHAT DOES COPYRIGHTING PROTECT?

Copyrighting, a form of intellectual property law protects original works of authorship including literary, dramatic, musical, and artistic works, such as poetry, novels, movies, songs, computer software, and architecture.

HOW IS A COPYRIGHT DIFFERENT FROM A PATENT OR A TRADEMARK?

Copyright protects original works of authorship, while a patent protects inventions or discoveries. Ideas and discoveries are not protected under the copyright law, although the way in which they are expressed may be. A trademark protects words, phrases, symbols, or designs identifying the source of the goods or services of one party and distinguishing them from those of others.

IS COPYRIGHTING MANDATORY?

No. It is voluntary. You will have to register your work if you wish to bring a lawsuit to prove that someone stole it, though.

IS MY COPYRIGHT GOOD IN OTHER COUNTRIES?

The United States has copyright relations with most countries throughout the world, and as a result of these agreements, we honor each other's citizens' copyrights. However, the United States does not have such copyright relationships with every country.

For more information on copyrighting, go to www.copyright.gov/help/faq/. To register your work for copyrighting, visit http://copyrightregistry-online-form.com/.

Module 4 Tip 6:
Your Copyright Page

Your copyright page will have the copyright symbol ©, date of publication, the words, "first printing" with the year, credit to the cover designer and proofreader (if applicable), the ISBN number and your legal disclaimer. On the next pay are some examples of copyright pages. As you will see, I was a little creative and decided to list my other books on this page.

The copyrighting page This page carries the copyright disclaimer, edition information, publication information, printing history, cataloging data, legal notices, and the book's ISBN or identification number. In addition, rows of numbers are sometimes printed at the bottom of the page to indicate the year and number of the printing. Credits for design, production, editing, and illustration are also commonly listed on the copyright page.

Things that Must be on the Copyright Page

The single most important element on the copyright page is the copyright notice itself. It usually consists of three things:

    1. the © symbol, or the word "Copyright"
    2. the year of first publication of the work
    3. an identification of the owner of the copyright: author's name, abbreviation, or some other way that it's generally known.

Together, it should look like this:

Module 4 Tip 7:
Publication Date

Books are often available months before their publication date. This is called a "preview". If you finish a book after September, my advice is to list the publication date for the coming year. In other words, if your book is completed in October 2013, make the publication date on your copyright page for 2014. That way the book will seem more recent. Otherwise, it will only seem recent for two months because when the next year rolls around, your book will seem old. The last book that I wrote, 'The Cost of the Anointing' was completed in October of 2012, but it is registered and copyrighted for 2013. That way it looked recent all year long.

Module 4 Tip 8:
Have an Eye-catching book cover or title

PEOPLE BUY BOOKS FOR ONE OF THREE REASONS:

1. AUTHOR
2. TITLE
3. COVER

For some, it does not matter what the title of the book is or what the cover of the book looks like. They will buy the book simply because their favorite author wrote it. When you get a loyal following, you will acquire loyal fans and your loyal fans will buy books based upon your name alone. If your name is not well-known as yet, then your book should have a catchy and compelling title that will draw people to it. Developing a good title for your book helps ensure that it will stick in the minds of prospective readers. A good book title is considered a marketing tool for your book. Your book's title should create an emotional response in your potential readers.

If your title is not very catchy, then you at least want a stimulating, eye-catching book cover. You need at least one of the three (name, catchy title, eye-catching cover). Wouldn't it be great to have all three? Try to make your title catchy and compelling so that readers will want to pick up your book to see what's inside. If you do not have a title for your book as yet, you may choose a "working title". You may end up changing that title several times before finishing the book.

Module 4 Tip 9:
Your book can have babies!

You can make workbooks for your books with matching covers. The covers for your workbooks may be the EXACT same matching covers as your books. The only difference is that the workbooks are 8 ½ by 11 or larger in size and they say W O R K B O O K on the front cover. When/if you do decide to develop a workbook to accompany your book, you already have the matching cover!

You may also take chapters out of books and make a whole new book from those. For instance, I wrote a book called 'Life After High School' (LAH). The book is FILLED with information on a variety of subjects for young adolescents entering adulthood. After I wrote that book, I made four small books from the chapters in the big book and had them published. I simply added new and different covers, modified the content and gave them each a new ISBN. Once those things were complete, I had brand new books. For the most part, the books were already written. Out of LA came a money management book, a book on relationships, a military book, and a goal-setting book; so my book 'Life After High School' had four babies!

Module 4 Activity

1. What are the two parts of a book?

   _____

   _____

2. What are the three parts to a book cover ?

   i. _____

   ii. _____

   iii. _____

3. Your book cover should be converted into two formats. What are they?

   i. _____

   ii. _____

4. What is the old-fashioned way of creating your book cover?

   _____

   _____

   _____

5. What is an ISBN number and what is the purpose of it?

   _____

   _____

   _____

6. What is the difference between a copyright and a trademark? _____

_____

_____

7. Will you be copyrighting your book? ____yes ____no
   Why or why not? Please explain. _____

_____

_____

_____

_____

My Book Notes

Module 5

Uploading Your Files
Converting to a Portable Document Format

Once your book is ready to be printed, meaning it has been proofread, edited, typeset, formatted, covers are complete and the book looks and reads exactly how you want it to, then it's time for the conversion.

Your manuscript must be converted into a Portable Document Format (also known as Adobe PDF) before it can be uploaded and printed. The default in PDF must be changed from standard to high quality. Once converted, you must then review the new file page by page, carefully making sure that everything is still in place because sometimes during conversion, pages lose their formatting due to glitches (Trust me. I found out the hard way). You must absolutely take your time to ensure that each page has proper spacing, that pages did not jump up or down, and that page titles start on the correct side. This is very important because how your book looks on the PDF is how it will look in the hands of your readers. I have had to convert files five and six times because when reviewing the PDF version, something got misaligned, or I saw something in the PDF that I did not see on MS Word file.

When a page jumps, you must fix it in MS Word, convert the file to PDF again, then review page by page all over again. You must repeat this process until your file looks exactly how you want it to look. It is not so bad; it just takes an eagle's eye. If you are sleepy or tired, then wait until the next day to review the PDF page by page before uploading. Do not upload until you are extremely sure that each page is properly aligned.

Module 5 Tip 2
Uploading Your Files

You may be wondering where you upload to. You upload to the company you are using to publish or print your book. When you are self-publishing, printing and publishing sometimes may mean the same thing, but what distinguishes printing from publishing is that to publish your book means that your ISBN number is registered and your book can be found on the book trade market when it is looked up. Just because you print a book does not mean you have published a book.

What company you use to upload your book depends upon how much of the book creation process you were able to do on your own. For instance, if you have done your own typing, formatting, organizing, typesetting, proofreading, editing, acquiring of your own ISBN number, did your own book covers (with the help of maybe a graphic designer, editor, or some friends or family), then you are considered a "self-publisher" and you will upload to a **minimum-service** print on demand (POD) company. These companies take your completed PROOFREADY files and bound and print your book for you. You will upload your completed PDF covers and interior to these companies and they will process your files and send you a proof copy in the mail. Once you get your proof, you either approve or reject it, then you start ordering your copies! Some of these companies even register your books with big distribution companies such as Amazon, Ingram and Barnes and Noble.

If you do not have the necessary clerical skills and cannot do all of the things I listed above (typing, formatting, organizing, typesetting, proofreading, editing) on your own, then you will use a "**full-service** subsidy publisher" who will do almost everything for you except write your book. Full service subsidy publishers provide a whole range of things such as organizing, editing, proofreading, formatting, cover design, ISBN, the whole gamut.

64

Print on Demand companies will "print your books on demand."
They print books for you as you request them. They provide very
minimal services.

Module 5 Tip 3:
Full & Minimum Service Companies

If you need FULL services, such as typing, formatting, organizing,
editing, formatting, ISBN, copyrighting, graphic designing,
representative help - THE WORKS, then you will work with a full-
service subsidy publisher. In this case, they are your publisher and
you are the author. At this point, you are not self-publishing. They
will do 90% of everything for you except write your book, but they
can be expensive, starting at $1,000 and up.

With a MINIMUM service company, you can pay as low as $100.00
and some minimum service companies are cheaper than that; so if
you have the computer skills to put your own book together, then
use your skills to pay the bills!

The companies listed below provide minimum services to authors.
They are reputable print-on-demand companies. They will print your
proof ready book for you, but you should do your own research on
each company. To use their services, it is understood that your book
is ready to be printed (although a few of them provide formatting
and organizing such as Lulu). All of these companies will print your
books and distribute them, meaning they will put them on the book
trade market (Amazon, Ingram or Barnes and Noble). Call and/or
visit their websites to find out what they offer before choosing one
to work with.

Minimum Service Companies:

www.lightningsource.com (can convert your manuscript to ebook
and distributes it to Amazon, Barnes & Noble Ingram Distributors)

  ➢ www.createspace.com (can convert your manuscript to audio
    CD, MP3, DVD and video download and distributes to
    Amazon. They also produce full-color books. You can also
    create your covers on this site.)

> www.lulu.com (can convert your manuscript to ebook and distributes it to Amazon, Barnes & Noble & other retails cites, You can also create your covers on this site)

> www.booklocker.com (can convert your manuscript to ebook and distributes to Apple ibookstore, Amazon's kindle, & Barnes & Noble Ingram Nookbook store)

Module 5 Tip 4:
Subsidy (aka Vanity) Publishers

If you work with a subsidy publisher, they will walk you through the uploading process and anything else that you personally would need to do. But you must do your homework. Call them. Find out what they offer. Compare prices with other companies. Determine the best fit for you. The list below is in no particular order, but contains some subsidy (vanity) companies that can help publish your book.

FULL SERVICE SUBSIDY PUBLISHERS
www.booksurge.com (1.866.356.2154.)
www.dogearpublishing.com (1-888-568-8411)
www.iuniverse.com (1800-288-4677)
www.llumina.com (866-229-9244))
www.millcitypress.net (612-455-2294)
http://friesenpress.com (1-800-792-5092)
www.outskirtspress.com (1-888-672-6657)
www.dorrancepublishing.com (800) 695-9599)
www.outskirtspress.com (1-888-672-6657)
www.BookstandPublishing.com (1-866-793-9365)
www.Instantpublisher.com (1-800-259-2592)
www.morrispublishing.com (1-800-650-7888)
www.virtualbookworm.com (877-376-4955.)
www.xulonpress.com (specializes in Christian's books) (1-866-381-2665)
www.tatepublishing.com (specializes in Christian's books) (888- 361-9473

* Before doing business with a subsidy publishing company (aka vanity company), do a Google search to check out the company. For example, search for: The company name + scam; The company name + fraud; The company name + rip off; The company name + better business bureau.

When calling these companies, ask questions such as the ones below and think of some of your own that meet your personal needs:

1. Will you be able to distribute my books to any of the following distributors?: Ingram, Barnes and Noble, and/or Amazon?
2. Do you provide e-book conversions?
3. What book sizes to you offer?
4. Do you provide professional editing services?
5. Do you have cover layouts from which to choose?
6. What is the approximate unit price that I will pay for my book? (You must give the number of pages and book size to them)
7. Do I get a proof copy of my book?
8. Do you provide services for children's books (if applicable)
9. Do I have to pay all at once?

PLEASE KEEP IN MIND THAT:
Limited or Full-Service companies require that you, the author pay all costs and they do not do any effective marketing or promotions for you. All marketing efforts are totally up to you. However, your signed contract with them may give the *impression* that considerable marketing work will be performed. More than likely, the smooth salesperson will, without making any real promises, lead you to believe that the vanity publisher will make a considerable effort to market your title. You will pay the costs (usually inflated) of editing, design, production, and printing. You are led to believe that the publisher will "take care of everything" for you. They will make you believe that you will not have to do anything to sell your book while not putting that in writing. You must keep these things in mind when

67

working with these companies. Don't be fooled into believing that they are going to put all of their time, energy and effort into making you a number one best seller because they will not. They want your business, but the marketing efforts must come from you.

If your book has a very limited market such as a family history book, then that is likely to appeal only to members in your family. In a case like that, these "publishers" will be a waste of money.

Module 5 Tip 5:
Receiving Your Proof in the Mail

After you upload your PDF file, it will take a couple of days before you will be notified that it has been processed and approved. Once processed, you will be sent a proof copy of your book in the mail. There is nothing more exciting than opening up a UPS or Fedex package that contains your 1st book - the book YOU wrote. I have written 15 books and I am still excited when a new one arrives in the mail. That is just the way it is, but…

despite how many times you have corrected errors before uploading or how good the editor was, you WILL see errors in the book when you get the proof back. I do not know why that is, but you will see mistakes in the book that neither you, nor the editor saw on the computer. That is fine because they are easier to correct with the proof copy in your hand. It does not take any of the excitement away because 99% of the process is done!

Module 5 Tip 6:
Lightning Source

I use Lightning Source to print and distribute my books on the book trade market. In order to use this company, your book must be completely finished, and all that needs to be done is to have it bound and printed.

After you get your proof in the mail, you must approve it online. You will not be able to order additional books until you approve the proof.

Once you make changes from your proof copy to the original file, you will upload a second time then begin ordering your inventory. Now that your book is totally complete, you must also make sure that it is being distributed on the book trade market for all distributors to see that a new book has been released and ready for purchase. Therefore, the next thing that must be done is to ensure that your distribution strategies are effective, which we will now cover in the next module.

Module 5 Activity

1. Do you have the clerical skills to type and organize your own manuscript? ___yes ___no

2. Do you already have a company in mind to use yet? _____

If so, list the service they offer that will help you in this process.

    a. _____

    b. _____

    c. _____

    d. _____

    e. _____

3. Will you need a minimum service company or a full service company to help you with your book? Explain.

_____

_____

_____

4. List the things that you will need help with in publishing your book (ex. typing, formatting, organizing, etc.).

    a. _____

    b. _____

    c. _____

d. _____

e. _____

5. List the things that you can do on your own with your creation of your book. ex. typing, formatting, organizing, etc.).

    a. _____

    b. _____

    c. _____

    d. _____

    e. _____

6. Will you need a consultant to help you through the process? ___yes ___no

7. Have you begin writing your book yet? If so, how much near completion are you? ___10 % ___25% ___50%

    ___75% ___85% ___100% ___0%

My Book Notes

_____

_____

_____

_____

_____

_____

_____

_____

_____

_____

_____

_____

_____

_____

_____

_____

_____

_____

_____

_____

_____

_____

_____

_____

Module 6
Distribution
Getting lots of online Exposure for Your Book

Ancillary publishing is having your book for sale on the book-trade market in days! Your words, your title, your cover in print and marketed by an experienced publisher costing you little of nothing!

There are at least five ancillary publishers that are eager to put your words, images, and artwork in print, as either a regular paperback book (like you see in bookstores) or an almost immediately accessible e-Book. You pick the publisher and they produce your book or you pick all five, and they will produce 7-10 different versions of your book!

After you upload your final file, your book should be ready for distribution and promotion. You should have your testimonials in (if you requested some), your foreword written (if you have one), all of your completed preliminary pages, and your book should be 99.5% error free and ready to be read by the world.

Module 6 Tip 2:
Distribution

The key to your book exposure will be getting your book in the book trade market by being in the inventory of the big book distributors. The top three book distributors in the United States are Ingram, Baker and Taylor (Barnes & Noble) and Amazon. This means that big bookstores, outlets or businesses that sell books, will get the books from one of these three major distributors (Baker and Taylor provides 95% of Barnes & Noble's books).

How do you get your books in the inventory of these big distributors you ask? Through secondary publishers such as the ones already mentioned: Lightning Source, Createspace, Lulu, etc. Through these companies, you get in through the back door of large distributors that would otherwise be unreachable unless you are a very well-known person and/or a best-selling author.

Module 6 Tip 3:
How does ancillary distribution work?

Once your book is ready, you will upload to different companies who all have access to big distributors and/or bookstores and/or potential buyers. They make their money by selling your books! Here's how it goes: You select them to publish your book, which they will sell. They will retain a percentage of the proceeds and send you the rest, which will be considered your royalties. You earn a modest piece of the pie.

What is the purpose of doing this?
The purpose of this is to get as much exposure for your book as possible by placing your book worldwide in the inventory of big book traders on the market and having it in different versions.

Which companies do you upload to and why?
You choose who you want to use. Below are some companies you may want to consider. Look at what they offer because they each offer different, but significant things. Most of them charge NOTHING to upload your book!

LIGHTNING SOURCE - Places your book with Amazon, Barnes & Noble, and Ingram distributors; provides paperback and hardback books, converts to e-book, are relatively inexpensive and your unit cost books are relatively inexpensive. (I have never paid over $4.50 for any of my books from them. I sell my books at $10.00, $15.00, $20.00 & $25.00) They also send you royalties every 90 days.

LULU - They market your books on their own marketplace through their social networks. Places your book with Amazon, Barnes & Noble distributors; produces CDs and DVDs in addition to books, provides paperback and hardback books, converts to e-Book, publishes in seven languages and sells in four listed currencies. They send you royalty checks.

CREATESPACE - This company is a subsidy of Amazon. They are a POD wing that funnels your book into production, then sells them primarily through the Amazon website. They send you royalty checks.

BLURB - They only sell through their online bookstore. Most people use them if they are writing a book that only their family and relatives will appreciate. People who write art books, travel, cookbooks, or baby books use blurb. Why should YOU use Blurb? Because they will sell your book on their website and pay you royalties every time your book sells. That's why!

KINDLE - Has the best known e-reader program. They are part of Amazon and are eager to include your books to be read on their reader. Inclusion costs you NOTHING! But a PDF upload won't work. However, they will convert your file for you. You will earn 35% per sale. Yes, they too will send you royalty checks!

SMASHWORDS/EBOOK
They pay you a whopping 85% of the net! They take your file and converts it into nine DRM-free e-book formats: EPUB (the open industry format), PDF (the best for holding content in place), RTF (rich text format), PDB (for palm pilots), MOBI (kindle), LRF (Sony reader), & TXT (plain text).

Which company should I buy my unit cost books from?
I recommend getting your inventory from Lightning Source (LS). These are the books that you are going to sell to family, friends and strangers and use for your book launch/signing. You should always have an inventory on hand. I keep my books in the trunk of my car. That way, they are with me wherever I go. You never know when

you will get an opportunity to sell. If you get low on inventory, you can place an order online at LS anytime night or day. You can order anywhere from 5, 25, 50, 100, 250 books, so on. There is no minimum amount to order. The average unit cost of my books range from 2.50 - 4.50 per book. The more books you order, the higher your discount. Your royalty from LS will not be much at first, but having them as your intermediary is a blessing. With LS, you do not have to stock or ship any books and you get a percentage of every book sold. How cool is that?

After you upload your files to those ancillary publishers for almost nothing, you have done more than 90% of what authors do after they write a book! Now your paperback and eBooks are available on Lighting Source, Lulu, Createspace, blurb, kindle and smashwords! You have many secondary publishers selling your book to bookstores and outlets that you did not have before, plus you have an inventory for your own use. I am so impressed with you!

Module 6 Tip 4:
Your Book Description

Before going to each of those websites to upload, you must already have your book description ready because they will request this. The book description is called an "annotation", so write it before hand. Your book description should be about 300 words long and should sound phenomenal! You must write it in a way that will make readers want to run to buy your book. This is important because reading the annotation will determine if people will buy your book or not. You will not be there to explain what the book is about, so the annotation/description does that for you.

Sample Chicago Manual Style Annotation

Davidson, Hilda Ellis. *Roles of the Northern Goddess*. London: Routledge, 1998.

Davidson's book provides a thorough examination of the major roles filled by the numerous pagan goddesses of Northern Europe in everyday life, including their roles in hunting, agriculture, domestic arts like weaving, the household, and death. The author discusses relevant archaeological evidence, patterns of symbol and ritual, and previous research. The book includes a number of black and white photographs of relevant artifacts.

This annotation includes only one paragraph, a summary of the book. It provides a concise description of the book's project and its major features.

Sample APA Annotation
Ehrenreich, B. (2001). *Nickel and dimed: On (not) getting by in America.* New York: Henry Holt and Company.

In this book of nonfiction based on the journalist's experiential research, Ehrenreich attempts to ascertain whether it is currently possible for an individual to live on a minimum-wage in America. Taking jobs as a waitress, a maid in a cleaning service, and a Walmart sales employee, the author summarizes and reflects on her work, her relationships with fellow workers, and her financial struggles in each situation.

An experienced journalist, Ehrenreich is aware of the limitations of her experiment and the ethical implications of her experiential research tactics and reflects on these issues in the text. The author is forthcoming about her methods and supplements her experiences with scholarly research on her places of employment, the economy, and the rising cost of living in America. Ehrenreich's project is timely, descriptive, and well-researched.

The annotation above both summarizes and assesses the book in the citation. The first paragraph provides a brief summary of the author's project in the book, covering the main points of the work. The second paragraph points out the project's strengths and evaluates its methods and presentation. This particular annotation does not reflect on the source's potential importance or usefulness for this person's own research.

It is a good idea to memorize your book description so when people ask you what your book is about, you have a ready-made answer. At this juncture, your book is finished, is 99.5% error-free, has been uploaded to ancillary publishers, and now you are ready to promote it.

Module 6 Tip 5:
Things to keep in mind:

* Distribution is what gets your books into the bookstores and ancillary publishing is the way to get them there.

* The books that ancillary publishers produce must look professional in appearance. Once the book is completed, you do the submitting (uploading).

* After the book is completed, you will do the rest at the submission level. Ancillary publishers will post your book for worldwide attention, make it available to major book distributors, sell it from their website, and (in some cases) link it to other sellers.
* To sell the most books, you must consider a 55% discount and full-return policy when setting up your account. If your discount amount is less than 55%, chances are most bookstores will not pick you up. Some compensation is better than no compensation.

* The unit cost that you pay per book depends upon how many pages the finished book will be and the trim size of the book (5x8, 5.5 x 8.0, 6x9, etc.) The more books you print, the less per-unit cost.

* 55% of books sold in the U.S. move through Ingram warehouses. Ingram Content Group is a United States-based service provider to the book publishing industry based in La Vergne, Tennessee. They have the industry's largest active book inventory with access to 7.5 million titles. The markets they serve include booksellers, librarians, educators, and specialty retailers.

* Your first book is a learning experience, but you still want a professionally designed, attractive cover with a selling title and is error-free and logically written.

* It is the printed book that makes the most money not the e-Book. As you know, your printed book must be designed, typeset, printed and bound. When you self-publish, YOU are the publisher.

Module 6 Activity

1. According to what you have learned, what does ancillary publishing mean?

_____

_____

_____

2. What is the benefit of ancillary publishing?

_____

_____

_____

3. Explain what an annotation means.

_____

_____

_____

4. How many ancillary publishers should you upload to? _____

5. How do you get your self-published books in the big bookstores?

_____

_____

_____

6. What companies can help you get your books onto Barnes & Nobles and Amazon websites?

_____

_____

_____

7. What does unit cost refer to?

_____

_____

8. Why should you memorize your book description?

_____

_____

9. On the lines below, write your book description that way you would say it to someone:

_____

_____

_____

_____

_____

My Book Notes

_____

_____

_____

_____

_____

_____

_____

_____

_____

_____

_____

_____

_____

_____

_____

_____

_____

_____

_____

_____

_____

_____

Module 7
Marketing Your Book
Creating a Buzz around
Your Book

Writing a book is relatively easy. The rest takes time, energy, and effort, but the reward is worth the effort. Stores want authors who sell books. Books don't sell themselves. Authors must sell them, therefore, the book promotion and marketing part is up to YOU. You may have the best-written, most informative and professional-looking book ever, but if no one knows about it, then what's the point? You may also have a book filled with grammatical, spelling and punctuation errors that is poorly written, but it's a number one seller. What's the difference? PROMTION AND MARKETING!

The average author sells no more than 100 books during the book's lifespan. Writing a book is 10%. The other 90% comes from marketing and promotion. A book has four stages that it goes through:

1. Creation
2. Production
3. Distribution
4. Promotion

When a book fails to sell, it is because it was not effectively taken through all four stages. Promotion is mandatory if you expect people to buy your book! If you are the writer, the publisher and the marketer, then book promotion is up to YOU. In order to effectively do these things, you must have a marketing strategy. Do you have one? Hmmmm. Something to think about.

Module 7 Tip 1:
Reminders

We will begin by reviewing some basic ways you can begin to promote and market your book. Later we will get into some nontraditional ways, but for now, let me just give you a list of reminders and/or seeds that will start you off with your promotion piece.

1. The title of your book must be compelling enough to target your readers and make someone want to pick up your book to find out more.

2. Your front cover should be eye-catching and stimulating.

3. Your back cover should give the benefits of reading your book. Your small professional- headshot can go in the back as well (if it's not on the front).

4. Your book must be thick enough to suggest that it is worth the price that you are selling it for, but not so thick that it will scare readers off.

5. Your book must be well-written, fully proofread, reliably researched, fit in with other books in its genre (inside and out) and contain useful, inspiring and significant information, a story, or whatever you are discussing.

6. Your book must be professional-looking.

7. Ancillary publishers provide professional-looking books. They expect you to have the knowledge, the words, and the skill to submit your two core files: the interior and the exterior.

8. Be able to answer the following question: How is your book is unique from other books in its genre?

9. You should have two descriptions of your book: a long one (about 300 words) and a short one (about 150 words). You should memorize the short one.

10. You must be thoroughly familiar with the content of your book. When you cannot answer questions about certain things written in your book, it makes people question your authenticity and credibility.

Module 7 Tip 2:
Things you can do to Promote your Book

1. Send out an Email Blast
When your book is almost finished (you are writing your last chapter or two), you can send out an email blast to family and friends introducing the book and including a pre-order form. For those of you who are not technologically savvy and (for whatever reason) do not have an email address, you may use the old-fashioned way of getting the word out - the telephone.

Presales serve two purposes. It announces the coming of your book and it gets you commitments from buyers. Example of a preorder form:

PREORDER FORM   **A Walking Miracle**

Author Patricia Johnson

NAME: _____ PHONE: _____

ADDRESS (include City, State, Zip): _____

_____

e-mail address: _____

How many books would you like? _____ $15.00 x _____ = $_____
Please Make Checks payable to Patricia Johnson or "CASH"

_____ Please mail the books to the above address (add $3.00 for shipping)
_____ I will arrange to pick up the book from you

If you do not already have a website, you may buy your domain name at www.godaddy.com. Domain names are as cheap at 4.99 flat rate depending on the name you choose. You can use vistaprint.com or godaddy.com to build your site, or you can use www.web.com to help create the site for you. Vistaprint is the least expensive I've encountered and their sites are user friendly. Many companies can help you build a functional website. You may also use college students majoring in graphic design to do it for you. Pack your website with information pertaining to your book including excerpts. Have a jpeg (picture) of the cover, your professional photo headshot, a video of you in an interview (if applicable), links to any coverage in magazines, radio, newspapers, articles and/or other online outlets, a list of topics you can discuss, and of course your immediate contact information. On your website, you should also have a well-written bio that showcases your credentials, experience and education for writing a book. Your top credentials are listed first, then your education, special areas of expertise and then follow with your accomplishments, awards etc. Include impressive media you have secured (if applicable) to show that you are well-credentialed and experienced. Include testimonials of people who have read your book and put them on your website. Try and get some well-known names.

3. Have a Book Launch

Your book launch can be on a small, medium or large scale. Keep in mind that the purpose of the Book Launch is to announce your book to everyone with hopes that they will buy them. In other words, you don't just want to offset the cost of having the launch (venue, food, decorations, etc.) with the books you sell. You want to make money from the sales and make a profit. By having a launch, you are introducing the world to your book for the second time (the first time was when you uploaded to five ancillary publishers).

You may have this signing at someone's home, a clubhouse, or go big and do it at a hotel or banquet hall. It's up to you and your pocketbook. At your signing, you will read excerpts from your book and answer any questions that your guests may have. At the signing, you can have index cards at the entrance table where people will write their names and what they want you to write in their book after they buy it. When it's book signing time, they will hand you the index card with their name and you will write what's on the index card in the book.

A book launch is a familiar way of coming out of the closet with your book and letting everyone know about it. While at the signing, also inform guests of the different versions in which your book may be available (e-book, a-book, pbook, Hbook, MP3, etc.).

Have someone other than yourself take money. You will be at the end of the table signing while the books are displayed at the front and middle of the table. You should not have to worry about money, giving change, etc. Your job is to talk about your book, read excerpts, give information, then autograph the copies that people buy. Be prepared to answer questions such as:

> 1. What made you write this book?
> 2. How long did it take you to write it?
> 3. If it is a novel, be prepared to answer questions about characters such as, "Are they real people?"

Module 7 Tip 3:
Word-of-mouth is the best advertisement!

When you tell enough people about your book, and they read it and tell others, and those people tell others, you will definitely sell more books! If you wrote a children's book, you may inform the local library, childcare centers in your neighborhood and local schools. You may volunteer to go and read to the students as well. You are getting the word out about your book this way and the library is always looking for new books to add to their collection. Your next networking strategy is to inform local organizations in your category about your book. In planning for this, you may sit down and make two lists for your book:

1. organizations that you are a part of (church, sorority/fraternity, civic, community, etc.)

2. Organizations that you are not a part of, but know of in your book

category (associations, clubs, magazines, catalogues, events/conventions, forums, online social networks).

Set up an appointment to meet the leaders of these organizations and offer discounts for bulk
purchases. You may also network over the internet by searching for organizations interested in your book's topic.

Module 7 Tip 4:
Your Brochure/Business Card

Have a vibrant brochure with the title of your book, your name as the author and the book cover on the brochure. You may get inexpensive, but quality-looking business cards from www.vistaprint.com. They are always having great deals and they sell other promotional items. I get 90% of my promotional products from them. Every time you tell someone about your book, give them a business brochure.

Module 7 Tip 5:
Get Local Exposure for Your Book

Promoting your book locally is where you may start. Regional and national media will not be interested in you or your book until you have generated some local attention. It is much easier for new authors to gain attention from their local community before getting noticed abroad. Your book-signing is a good way to open that door.

Module 7 Tip 6:
Create a Media Kit

Compile information about your book that you may send to the media. Your media kit should include a pitch letter introducing yourself and your book, excerpts from your book or a copy of it, your bio and photo, any positive endorsements or reviews that you have received, sample interview questions for them to ask you, and any news articles or clippings related to your book's topic. Your media kit will be the first impression that editors, producers, reviewers or reporters have of you and your book, so make sure there are no spelling or grammatical errors.

Module 7 Tip 7:
Create a monthly newsletter

You can create a monthly newsletter focused around your book. Of course you will provide other information in your newsletter, such as quotes from other books and things going on in the month. For instance, if it is the month of February, your newsletter can be red with hearts on it or around the border and you may give information on love and relationships, but you will always highlight your book, excerpts from your book or give a special discount in your newsletter for those who purchase the book during a certain timeframe. You may use incentives by saying something like, "The first 10 people who order the book will be mentioned in next month's newsletter." A wonderful website that provides newsletter templates, allows you to do email marketing, social campaigns, online surveys and even create events is www.constantcontact.com. Another website that is useful for creating newsletters is http://www.mynewsletterbuilder.com/. Those are a great place to start. Printshop also has a variety of newsletter templates from which to choose.

If you do no not have a large email database, then now is the time to start building it. You should already have email addresses of family and friends. A quick and easy way to build your database is by uploading your facebook contacts to your email address book by going to this website and following the instructions. http://www.facebook.com/find-friends. These are the people to whom you will send your newsletters and emails introducing your book.

Module 7 Tip 8:
Conduct Workshops/Trainings/Seminars

Why not convert your book into a how-to workshop, training, seminar or conference and offer to clubs, youth groups, churches, organizations, associations or through college or university programs? You may include your book as part of the registration fee. Figure the cost of the venue, the food (if applicable), the set up, the materials, handouts, (bags) and the audio visual. From that, you determine how many participants you will need to offset the cost, then add the cost (or a discounted cost) of your book and give everyone a copy as part of their registration fee. See the link below to find out how to start your own seminar. www.setupandmarketyourownseminar.com/ Workbooks would go really well with this.

Module 7 Tip 9:
Mini Seminars

Offer a mini-seminar at a local bookstore on your book's subject, but you must turn out the crowd. The store usually will provide the venue for free, but they want you to bring them new customers. If your event is successful, they will put your book in their stores. Go to the next chain store. Based on your prior performance, they will want you as well.

Each store is profiled. They know what will sell in their neighborhood. A business book will go in downtown stores while parenting and relationships books will go in the suburbs.

Module 7 Tip 10:
Pitch Story Ideas

The media wants a story, not a book. Many authors make the mistake of thinking that just because they have written a book, that will get them in the door for a book review or interview. NOT! The media wants a STORY. Talk shows want a STORY. Oprah wants a STORY. If you were adopted as a child and you later found your biological parents and you wrote a book about it, then that can turn into a great STORY to get you on a talk show, radio, or TV. Of course your book will come up during the interview, but it's not the book that gets you in the door, it's your story.

If you can provide some valuable and meaningful information that may benefit the community centered around your book, then you will be more likely to get an interview. Your book will come up in the interview, but you do not want to make the mistake of talking about your book every two minutes during the interview. You will turn people off and it will be obvious that you are self-promoting.

Most times you may provide the interviewer with questions to ask you beforehand. The questions will usually start off pertaining to the workshop, seminar, or conference that you are offering. Then, the interviewer may say, "You have also written a book right? Tell us a little about it?"

Module 7 Tip 11:
Your Amazon Page

Your page on Amazon not only lists your book, but it sells it. Amazon's description field has a limit of four thousand characters, so use the characters to your best advantage. In the products description, mention previous editions and other books authored by you. If you did a great job with your back cover, then you may use the same wording on your Amazon page. To set up an Amazon page, go to https://authorcentral.amazon.com.

Module 7 Tip 12:
FREE Social Media Networking

The growth of the internet has been extremely advantageous to authors and publishers because it presents new forums to find targeted groups of people, build awareness of books, and make purchasing fast and easy. Are you using social media to your advantage? If you are a business person or an author who desires to sell books, then you should be using your social media profiles to develop a brand for yourself (we will talk more about branding later). How are you presenting yourself on Facebook? Twitter? Linked-in? What are you saying that will make people want to know more about you, read your book or anything else you write for that matter?

Social media-networking can work for you if you strategically work it to your best interest. Be careful because it can also be used to hurt you. The top five networking sites in the world in order are 1. Facebook 2. Twitter 3. Linked-in 4. Myspace 5. Googleplus. They are all FREE social-media networking (advertising) sites. It's all in HOW you use them to your benefit. You simply cannot get a new social profile today and start advertising your books tomorrow. Who's going to buy your book? They don't know you. You must first create a presence, then develop your brand. You will eventually become known by your brand. Stay visible in the social networking world, then gradually present your book.

If you have several social media profiles, then there is a way to manage them all at one time, in one place at the click of a button through a website called www.hootsuite.com. My most active sites are Facebook, Twitter and Linked-in. It may seem that I am on these sites every day, but the truth is that I sometimes don't check them for days at a time (including FB), but you would never know because something is posted by me on each of my profiles daily. Hootsuite allows you to manage your profiles all in one place and schedule posts in advance by minutes, hours, days, weeks, and months. This way, you are not on the computer all the time, but are still connected to the social networking world. You still have a presence and a brand while doing other things. This is a way for you to create a brand around your book. Be strategic. I use hootsuite to manage all my profiles in one place and at one time. It allows up to five social media sites for free and after that. There is a monthly fee. Fees may vary, but I pay $9.99 monthly.

Module 7 Tip 13:
Contact Barnes & Noble directly

You may contact Barnes and Noble directly to ask them to consider putting your book in their stores. You will need to send the following three things when requesting consideration. 1. One copy of the finished book 2. Brief letter of intent (why should Barnes and noble stock your book?) 3. marketing plan. Everything needs to be sent in one package to the following address: Barnes & Noble/Small Press Department Marcella Smith, Vendor Relations 122 Fifth Avenue New York, NY **phone:** 212-807-0099 **phone:** 212-253-0810.

Module 7 Tip 14:
Write Articles

Not everyone is a writer, but some people have remarkable stories and they hire ghostwriters to write their stories for them because writing is not their strong point. There is nothing wrong with that, but if you ARE a writer, you may begin submitting online articles for free. All you do is take a page from your book, give it a title, introductory paragraph and submit the body. Always sign the end of your articles like this: "Extracted from (title of your book), copyright © 2013, (your name and your website address).

With these sites, you create a profile with your bio and include a link to your books. If readers like what you have to say in your article, they may just want to click on the link and buy your book. The top two free article websites are www.ezinearticles.com and www.articlesbase.com. Ezine only allows you to submit a certain number of articles for free, but afterwards, you must pay. With articlesbase, there is no limit and its free. See an article written by me and submitted online at the link below through articlesbase: http://tinyurl.com/atszuox

Module 7 Tip 15:
Start a Blog

As mentioned before, not all authors are writers, but if you like to write, you may want to consider creating a blog to develop a stronger online presence. Blogs are usually hosted by one person and contains his or her written thoughts, observations and "expert" opinions on a particular subject. Most blogs invite comments in order to get discussions going. As Dan Poynter states in his self publishing manual Volume 2 (2012) that, "Some authors are using blogs very effectively to build communities around subject matter of their books." However, you do not have to feel obligated to start a blog. Only start one if it is appealing to you and you are able to maintain it and direct traffic to it.

Some of the sites you may visit to create a blog are the following:

www.blogger.com
www.blogspot.com
www.wordpress.com
www.tumblr.com
www.posterous.com

Module 7 Tip 16:
Blog Talk Radio

If you like to talk and give information, blogtalk radio is a great way to promote your book. Blog talk radio was launched in 2006 and attracts nearly two million listeners a month. The system allows users to field phone calls, upload music, and effectively run a live radio show that can be archived. The free service makes its money by selling advertising. To start your own blogtalk, see the website below: www.blogtalkradio.com

Module 7 Tip 17:
Your Email Signature

Your email signature should promote you and your books and should have a link for people to click and buy your books. All these little subliminal things keeps the seeds planted in people's minds about your book and helps to strengthen your brand. Below is my email signature:

Mia Y. Merritt, TV Host
Author/Professional Speaker
www.miaymerritt.com
African American Achiever Recipient, JM
Family Enterprise (2011)
South Florida's 25 Most Influential &
Prominent Black Women in Business and
Leadership Recipient (2013)
http://www.facebook.com/merrittmia
http://twitter.com/#!/MiaMSays
Please click below to purchase a copy of my new book,
'The Cost of the Anointing'
http://bit.ly/16NDBHy

~ Conceive it, believe it. Take steps to achieve it; then leave the rest to God and prepare to receive it!

Module 7 Tip 18:
Put Yourself on YouTube

You tube has significantly grown and cannot afford to be ignored. Even if you only have one video of yourself on YouTube, it could be very beneficial for you. This can be an interview via TV or radio or it can simply be you teaching and/or giving valuable information. If you video yourself doing something positive, it is very simple to upload it to YouTube. Just go to www.youtube.com to create an account and follow the steps.

Module 7 Tip 19
WHAT IS A BRAND?

I have been talking a lot about building your brand and some may be wondering exactly what a brand is. Branding is the image that you want to be in the minds of people when they hear "your name." Branding is the connection that people make to what you do when they hear your name. The thing that they immediately connect you with when your name is mentioned is your BRAND!

Who's the brand?
When you brand yourself, YOU become the most valuable asset. You are the brand! You decide how you want yourself to be represented.

Not everyone knows who you are. Therefore, as you brand yourself, you will become known for what you do, what you say, and how you present yourself and your skills. Essentially, you are leaving a legacy!

What makes an effective brand?
Success and consistency in what you do overtime creates your brand. Connecting your name to your book, your field, product, or message is what makes your brand. Influencing how others perceive you and turning that perception into opportunity is strategic branding. Being UNIQUE and MEMORABLE enhances your brand!

What are the benefits in personal branding?

Personal branding gets your name out there, but YOU control how it gets circulated and what's attached to it. If you play your cards right, it establishes you as an expert in your field, which can lead to consulting opportunities centered around your book. Branding is a professional alter ego strategically designed to control what people think of you. It is not about who you know. It's about who knows you!

Increase your value.

Become the Expert in Your Field. Books, workbooks, CDs, You Tube, Workshops, Seminars Audio Books, Blogs, Video Emails - all the things you have read thus far helps to create a brand for you.

Promoting your book is not a task that will be completed overnight. The fruits of your efforts will not be immediately noticeable, but in time, your hard work will pay off. It takes time and persistence to get your book noticed. Celebrate every achievement and keep moving forward. The majority of books that ended up on the New York Times Best Seller had been released at least two years before they reached that level. Some books however, because of the well-known author become number one immediately after they are released. That's not very likely right now for people like you and I, but it is NOT impossible. Harry Potter is a good example.

Become a socially relevant author/expert to optimize your book promotion and publicity. Learn how to tie you and your book's messages into the news of the day. The idea is to expand yourself as an author and apply your knowledge and wisdom to the issues of interest to society today. All it takes is a little bit of time, commitment and dedication each day.

Module 7 Tip 20:
Create your Marketing Plan

Here are five tips for developing a basic marketing plan that can be applied to activities such as a book launch or promotional campaigns.

1. Build a Precise Picture of Your Ideal Customer

Identifying your target market is the first step towards any marketing plan and it is essential that you are as precise as possible about your market. If not, you run the risk of a scattergun approach that will dilute your message and drain your budget. Instead, think about your target market in terms of specifics. For instance, who in your current customer base is the right fit for your product or service? What other kinds of books do they purchase? Do their purchasing patterns suggest they might be a good target? How will you reach new customers outside of your customer base?

The more specific you are, the easier it will be to craft the right message and tactics for reaching that audience.

2. Know what you want to accomplish

Again, be specific. Stating that you want to increase brand awareness about your book is not specific enough. Think about what actions you want potential customers to take after they are made aware of your book or promotional activity. There may be multiple actions that you want them to take. For example, a webinar could be positioned as a free training opportunity and your initial goal would be to get your target market to register for the webinar. However, once it is over, you want to offer a special discount for your book in order to attract sales. For example: discounted price of the book if purchased within the next 24 hours.

3. Know Your Target Audience

As an author, it is very important to be able to identify your book's target audience. Many authors make the mistake of thinking that everyone is a potential reader, when in reality, some people are less likely to purchase your book than others. You must know your audience in order to target them. Would your book appeal more to females or males? What age range best represents your readers? What kind of activities do your readers pursue? The more you can narrow your focus, the easier it will be to locate your target audience and promote your book. Below are some questions that will be asked of you pertaining to your book:

97

1. Who is your target audience?
2. To what age range are you writing?
3. How can your book help readers?
4. What is unique about your book?
5. What are some other books written that are similar to yours?
6. What other versions is your book offered?

Now that you know who you want to reach and what actions you want them to take, you will need to identify the best ways to reach them and with what message. To do this, consider the following about your customers and prospects:

1. To what associations do they belong?
2. Are they active on social media?
3. Do they subscribe to your email marketing?
4. What print or online media do they read?
5. What are their pain points (how can you help address these)?
6. What types of messages or calls to action have they responded to in the past?
7. Why should they care about what you have to offer (what's in it for them and in what ways will they benefit)?

4. Plan Your Marketing Budget
When it comes to planning your budget, start with a figure that you can afford. Prioritize. Decided where you need to put your advertising efforts that will get you the most and best return.

5. Plan Your Strategies
Your strategies are the actions you need to take to help you reach your target market and accomplish your goals. These include specifics such as direct mail, email marketing, print/radio/online advertising, blogs, social media, webinars, teleseminars, events, sponsorships and so on.

Never rely on one strategy alone. An integrated approach that delivers a consistent message across multiple, targeted platforms is the best way to ensure you reach your target market and get the most out of your budget. Refer back to "who" it is you are trying to reach, where they are, and what you want them to do.

Above all, be flexible. Track results and adjust your strategy and plan of action when necessary. Try new and different email subject lines, test social media messages and keep a close eye on what works and what doesn't.

Do not forget a call to action: whether it is taking advantage of a coupon or attending an event. Use a unique code for each medium so that you may track where your leads are coming from.

Module 7 Tip 21:
Identify Your Niche

Niche Publishing is all about getting out the book in you and finding your niche. You have a book in you. It will appeal to a niche market as small as your family or as big as the world. Wherever you are in the process, your instinct will guide you through any or every one of the steps along the way.

Module 7 Activity

1. A book has four stages that it goes through. What are the four stages?

   _____

   _____

   _____

   _____

2. What should your title and/or your book cover be eye-catching and stimulating?

   _____

   _____

3. If you already know what you are going to write about, then write five or six bullets that will go on the back cover of your book. For instance: As a result of reading this book, readers will:

   _____

   _____

   _____

   _____

   _____

   _____

4. Name at least five marketing strategies that you will use to promote your book

      i. _____

      ii. _____

      iii. _____

      iv. _____

      v. _____

5. Are you on social media? If so, which sites will you strategy use to create your brand?

      i. _____

      ii. _____

      iii. _____

6. An email signature is a good way to keep the seed planted in people's minds about your book and/or what you do when you send or reply to emails. On the lines below, write a new email signature that helps with your brand.

_____

_____

_____

_____

_____

7. What will be your brand? In other words, what you do you want people to connect you with when they hear your name?

_____

_____

_____

8. Who is your target audience and where and how will you find them to get them to purchase your book? _____

_____

_____

9. What are you willing to spend money on to promote/market your book?

_____

_____

10. What is your ultimate goal for your book? _____

_____

_____

My Book Notes

Epilogue

It is my hope that this book has been a useful guide in providing you with the information and necessary tools that you will need to get you started on your book-writing journey. Writing a book is relatively a simply process. The hardest part of it is getting the book out of your head and into your hand. Knowing how to go about the book publishing process and understanding what is expected, what is appropriate, and what is not considered standard or professional plays an integral part in ensuring that your book is counted among those that are "quality".

You have a book inside of you and it is my goal to help you get it out. If this book has motivated you to get started, then my writing it was not in vain. Good luck in giving birth to your book and have a smooth journey along the way!

Dr. Mia Y. Merritt

Glossary of Terms

CPSIA information can be obtained at www.ICGtesting.com
Printed in the USA
LVOW12s2113120814

398745LV00001B/36/P

9 781631 736704